THE THINGS WE KNOW

THE THINGS WE KNOW

by

OSWALD J. SMITH, D.D., LL.D.

Foreword by
CHARLES T. COOK, D.D.

London
MARSHALL, MORGAN & SCOTT
Edinburgh

LONDON
MARSHALL, MORGAN & SCOTT, LTD.
1–5 PORTPOOL LANE
HOLBORN, E.C.1

AUSTRALIA
119 BURWOOD ROAD
MELBOURNE, E.13

SOUTH AFRICA
P.O. BOX 1720, STURK'S BUILDINGS
CAPE TOWN

CANADA
EVANGELICAL PUBLISHERS
241 YONGE STREET
TORONTO

THE PEOPLES PRESS
100 BLOOR EAST
TORONTO

U.S.A.
WORLD LITERATURE CRUSADE PRESS
BOX 1313, STUDIO CITY
CALIFORNIA

First published 1957
Second impression 1958

MADE AND PRINTED IN GREAT BRITAIN BY PURNELL AND SONS, LTD.
PAULTON (SOMERSET) AND LONDON

FOREWORD

By Dr. Charles T. Cook
Editor of *The Christian,* London

GOD has given Oswald J. Smith a remarkable ministry, both in Canada and in other lands. No ordinary man could attract congregations of two thousand people, week by week, in the same building, for twenty-five years, but that is the record of The Peoples Church, Toronto. Even his exceptional gifts as a speaker would not have accomplished this if it were not that he has the passion of the evangelist, the world vision of a missionary enthusiast, and the true pastoral heart. No wonder he has the respect and love of his flock.

Multitudes of men and women have been led to the Lord through his preaching. Everywhere he goes (and he has made many world tours) he presses upon the churches their responsibility for world evangelization. God did not satisfy his desire as a young man to go as a missionary to heathen lands. It would seem to have been the divine purpose to use him as one of the most successful pleaders for world missions in our time. His own people have caught much of his enthusiasm, for The Peoples Church contributes towards the support of over three hundred and fifty missionaries in all the five continents. What other church can equal that achievement?

Here in this book—the latest of the twenty-two he has published—we have a fair sample of Dr. Smith's pulpit ministry. His utterances have that prophetic quality which distinguishes all effective preaching. He does not philosophize about the Gospel, as some preachers do; he proclaims it. He never forgets that he is God's herald. He is an ambassador for Christ. "Thus saith the Lord" is the keynote of every message.

Having this conviction he feels impelled, like the Apostle Paul, to use "great plainness of speech", especially when he exposes the errors of some modern religious cults, or solemnly warns about the danger of judging others. Nevertheless, running through all his addresses is the tender compassion of a Christian spirit, yearning over the lost, and seeking to bring believers into ever closer fellowship with Christ.

I gladly respond to the request of my friend for a Foreword to this book. It is more than twenty years since I made his acquaintance, and I have had the privilege of visiting The Peoples Church on several occasions, of addressing the great congregations which gather there, and of seeing other features of this flourishing cause.

CHAS. T. COOK.

London, England.

CONTENTS

GOD UNDERSTANDS

Oswald J. Smith

B. D. Ackley

Slowly, with expression

1. God un-der-stands your sor-row, He sees the fall-ing tear,
2. God un-der-stands your heart-ache, He knows the bit-ter pain;
3. God un-der-stands your weak-ness, He knows the tempt-er's pow'r;

And whis-pers, "I am with thee," Then fal-ter not, nor fear.
O, trust Him in the dark-ness, You can-not trust in vain.
And He will walk be-side you How-ev-er dark the hour.

REFRAIN

He un-der-stands your long-ing, Your deep-est grief He shares;

Then let Him bear your bur-den, He un-der-stands, and cares.

CHAPTER I

THE CHRIST OF CHRISTMAS

NEARLY two thousand years ago there was born in Bethlehem of Judea, a Babe whose life was destined to affect countless millions. That Babe was Jesus Christ.

The time was ripe for His birth. Roman roads had been built throughout the civilized world in preparation for the feet of His future messengers. The Greek language had become almost universal in readiness for the proclamation of His Gospel.

The people among whom He was born were poor and despised, having been conquered by the Roman power. In the heart of every man was a cry for deliverance.

The world knew not of His birth. Work went on as usual. There was no tremendous upheaval announcing a new order. Kings and Potentates continued to rule as before. Nothing outwardly heralded His advent into the world.

Only Heaven appeared to be interested. In fact, God had to arrange a welcome Himself, and so legions of angels circled the skies and heralded His birth. Wise men from the East, studying the stars, and observing an unusual phenomenon in the heavens, came with their gifts from afar. Shepherds bowed in adoration and worship.

Rulers learned of His birth and became fearful and afraid. Anger filled their hearts. Murder was conceived and executed. Fearful of losing their power, they sought His death by every possible means.

Every diabolical plan that satanic ingenuity could devise was used to destroy Him. Demons trembled. Satan became enraged. All hell was allied against Him. But God was watching and He lived in spite of all.

He did not come to a palace with marble halls and carpeted stairs. No luxurious bed chamber was prepared for His birth. Neither nurses nor doctors were in attendance. Cathedral bells failed to toll; bands were silent; no royal choruses burst forth in song. Only the music of Heaven was heard. For He came to a stable, and He was laid in a manger. His mother had only the straw for a bed, and animals were her companions. There was no room in the inn.

Little did Caesar know that this Babe, through His teachings, would one day destroy his mighty Empire, bring to naught the majesty and power of Rome, and overthrow all earthly governments, or that the day would come when His birth, His life and His death would have a greater influence on humanity than the birth and death of any other man. For He was destined to be recognized by countless millions as the greatest of all the prophets, the mightiest of all the mighty, the Saviour of the world, God incarnate.

And now for nearly two thousand years His birth has been commemorated, for He is the central Figure of all history. More than nineteen hundred Christmas days have come and gone since that never-to-be-forgotten night when "the Word was made flesh and dwelt among us". And today, after the passing of more than nineteen hundred years, He is worshipped by countless millions, both dead and living, and untold multitudes are looking forward to the time when He will reappear "without sin unto salvation".

My friend, do you worship Him as your Saviour? Will you welcome Him when He returns? Have you accepted Him? If not, then do it, and do it—NOW.

CHAPTER II

FIVE THINGS YOU MUST KNOW

THERE are five things you must know in order to be saved. You may not know the Bible. You may not know theology. But these things you must know.

1. *You must know that you are a sinner in the sight of God*

The Bible says: "There is none righteous, no, not one" (Rom. 3: 10). If there are none righteous, then you are not righteous, and if you are not righteous, then you are a sinner. "All we like sheep have gone astray; we have turned every one to his own way" (Isa. 53: 6). "All" means all, therefore you are included. There are only two ways you can turn, your own way and God's way. If you have not turned God's way, then you have turned your own way, and if you have turned your own way, you have gone astray. If you have gone astray, then you are a sinner in the sight of God.

You are not a sinner because you sin, you sin because you are a sinner. An apple tree is not an apple tree because it bears apples, it bears apples because it is an apple tree. If you were an angel you would not sin, for angels do not sin. It is because you are a sinner that you sin.

You would not want to be rescued unless you knew you were drowning. You would not want food unless you knew you were starving. You would not want a doctor unless you knew you were sick. You will never want a Saviour until you know you are a sinner. Therefore you must know that you are a sinner first of all.

2. *You must know that your sins have been laid on Jesus*

The Bible says: "The Lord hath laid on him the iniquity of us all" (Isa. 53: 6). God had to deal with your sin before He could offer you salvation. An atonement had to be made. Jesus Christ made that atonement by bearing your sins in His own body on the tree and dying in your stead. Your sins were laid on Him. Jesus paid it all. He met the penalty, which was death, on your behalf. Sin was a great barrier between you and God. God had to tear down the barrier before He could deal with you in grace. He did that 1,900 years ago when He laid your sins on Jesus. Hence, He can now offer you mercy. Your sins are no longer on you; they are on the Lord Jesus Christ.

3. *You must know that you cannot save yourself*

"By grace are ye saved through faith; and that not of yourselves" (Eph. 2: 8) is what the Bible says. "Not of yourselves." You can no more save yourself than you can lift yourself by your own boot-straps. No man can be his own saviour. You cannot save yourself by getting yourself enrolled as a member of a church, or by getting yourself baptized. You cannot save yourself by turning over a new leaf and living a better life. You cannot save yourself by deeds of merit, or good works. There is nothing you can do to save yourself.

If you could save yourself, then the death of the Lord Jesus Christ was the greatest atrocity in the history of the world. You would not need Jesus Christ if you could be your own saviour. The very fact that Jesus died on Calvary for you proves conclusively that you cannot save yourself.

4. *You must know that Jesus Christ, and Jesus Christ alone, can save you*

"Thou shalt call his name Jesus: for he shall save" (Matt. 1: 21). "Neither is there salvation in any other, for there is none other name under heaven given among men, whereby we must be saved" (Acts 4: 12). "I am the way . . . no man cometh unto the Father, but by me" (John 14: 6). The Bible makes it perfectly clear, you see, that Jesus Christ, and Jesus Christ alone, can save you. No one else can.

5. *You must know that you must receive Jesus as your own personal Saviour*

No matter how much food you have, it will not save you from starvation unless you eat it. If you are dying of thirst, you must drink the water that is offered to you. If you have been bitten by a snake and you are dying of the poison, you must take the remedy for the poison.

"As many as received him, to them gave he power to become the sons of God" (John 1: 12). How do you become God's child? By receiving the Lord Jesus Christ as your own personal Saviour. That is the fifth thing you must know.

You must make a decision

Now, my friend, you know these five things, but what are you going to do? Are you going to act on your knowledge? Are you going to receive Jesus Christ as your Saviour? Are you prepared right now to invite Him into your heart? Will you take Jesus Christ today? The time has come for action. You must make a decision. You cannot drift into salvation. No one has ever been saved without making a decision.

That decision, my friend, should be made now. God says: "Now is the accepted time; behold, now is the day of salvation" (2 Cor. 6: 2). There is no tomorrow with God. It is now or never so far as He is concerned. He makes no promises for the future. You must accept Jesus Christ, and accept Him—NOW. Will you do it?

CHAPTER III

WHY NOT LIVE FOREVER?

WHY not live forever? You may, you know. The world's greatest Scientist says so. He states that He has "abolished death". He says He now has a life, available to all mankind, immune from death. He declares that "man may not die" but "live forever". All these statements you may read in His text book, 2 Timothy 1: 10, John 6: 50, 51, 58. Then, of course, in John 11: 26 we have that most startling pronouncement of His, "Whosoever liveth and believeth in me shall never die".

Long ago I believed what He said and trusted Him. Then I received that new and eternal life of which He speaks, and I now have the assurance that I will never die. I am going to live forever. Are you?

"Except a man be born again," He says, "he cannot see the Kingdom of God" (John 3: 3). Have you been born again? Are you alive? Remember, to be born once is to die twice, but to be born twice is to die but once, and that death is only physical. Having received His life, you yourself can never die. You are now immortal. You will live forever.

> *I take the life of Jesus Christ,*
> *'Tis all that I can do;*
> *The Holy Spirit recreates*
> *And I am born anew.*

Moreover, this life is a free gift. "The gift of God is eternal life through Jesus Christ our Lord" (Rom. 6: 23). There is no kind of a life you can live in order to get it. There is no church that can give it to you. Never can you become religious enough to obtain it. Nor will you ever be good enough to merit it. No works of yours can ever entitle you to it. "Not of works" (Eph. 2: 9), He says. It is God's gift through his Son, Jesus Christ, and you must receive it as you would any other gift, for you can never pay for it.

Then, too, it is found *only* in Christ, so that unless you take Him you will never possess it. "He that hath the Son hath life; and he that hath not the Son of God hath not life" (1 John 5: 12). That is why the Bible says, "As many as received him, to them gave he power to become the sons of God" (John 1: 12).

Hence, you must receive Jesus Christ, the crucified and risen Saviour, and when you do you will be saved, you will be God's child, you will have eternal life. Having saved you from the penalty of sin, which is death, He will then save you from the power of sin so that you may live a life of righteousness. Will you then receive Him?

The only reason you will die, remember, is because you refuse to live. "Ye *will not* come to me that ye might have life" (John 5: 40), He says. If you will come, He will give you the Life of the Ages and you will live forever. But if you refuse to come you will most assuredly die.

First, you will die physically. That is the death of the body. Then there is spiritual death. That is the death of the soul, and it is separation from God. Finally, there is eternal death. That is the death that never ends. It is separation from God forever and forever. Are you prepared to face it?

Oh, then, my friend, come! Close in with God's offer of mercy now, before it is forever too late. The issue is clear. It is between you and Christ. Will you accept or will you reject? It is for you to decide. Take Christ and you will live forever. Will you do it? Do it, and do it— NOW!

CHAPTER IV

MILLIONS ARE READING

D O you know that something has happened in this world of ours that has never happened before? Do you realize that for the first time in six thousand years people in large numbers are learning to read? Up until our generation, only a few have been able to read in comparison with the multitudes who have not. However, with the new methods that are now being used, people for the first time are able to read for themselves.

Do you know how many learn to read every week? You will be surprised when I tell you. No less than a million people every seven days learn to read for the first time. What does that mean? It means that a million who could not read a word last week are able to read this week. It means that another million who cannot read this week will be able to read next week.

Now what are they going to read? Of course they will read anything they can get their hands on. They are hungry for literature. Do you know what you would see if you were to visit the Asiatic world and look at the book-stands? You would see beautifully coloured magazines. Do you know what they are? They are the magazines of the Communists. The Communist presses are going day and night and they are turning out tons upon tons of literature. Very little of it is being sent to the Western world. Most of it goes to Africa and the different Asiatic countries. Why, they even claim that they won China by the printed page. Now they want to win the whole world. And they will do it unless the Church awakens before it is too late.

Do you know how many pieces of literature the Communists printed in one year? The Communists printed, within just one year, two pieces of literature for every man, every woman, every boy and every girl on the face of the earth. Can you tell me of any other nation that has printed that much for democracy? I know of none. The United States of America hasn't done it. Great Britain hasn't done it. But the Communists, as I have stated, have already printed two pieces of literature for every individual in the world. The Communists are on the job.

What else will you see on the bookstands? You will see another series of beautifully printed magazines. Do you know what they are? They are the magazines that are put out by Jehovah's Witnesses. Do you realize that Jehovah's Witnesses have one press, which is the largest religious press in the world, that runs night and day? Do you know how many magazines it prints every minute? It prints no less than 500 magazines per minute. That means 84,000,000 magazines a year. Where are these magazines distributed? They are sent to the Asiatic world, to Africa, and to many other countries. Jehovah's Witnesses provide literature for those who are learning to read for the first time. They are going to win them to their cult if at all possible.

Now, to a large extent, they are succeeding. They are baptizing hundreds while we are baptizing twos and threes. And every convert has been won by means of the printed page. They do not waste their money on luxurious church buildings. They do not build expensive churches and invite the people to come in. They put their money where it will count most for God. They put it into the printed page, into the message. They send their message out to those who do not have it, in an effort to reach them.

Let me tell you something. The Church of Jesus Christ is going to have to adopt some of the methods of Communism and those of Jehovah's Witnesses. Instead of building luxurious churches in which to worship God, we are going to have to put our money into the message and get the message out as far and as widely as possible.

Do you know how much money the Seventh Day Adventists put aside in one year for the printed page? You will be amazed when I tell you. They set aside $15,000,000. How much has your denomination set aside? I do not know of any other denomination in the world that sets aside $15,000,000 each year for the printed page. But the Seventh Day Adventists have done it. They know something of the power of the printed page and they are determined to get their message out.

My friends, I know of no other way by which we can carry out our Lord's command to reach "every creature" apart from the printed page. If the Church of Jesus Christ is going to use the methods that have been used for the last one hundred and fifty years it is going to fail. For a hundred and fifty years we have depended, more or less, on missionaries. Missionaries can never evangelize the world. It would be absolutely impossible for all the churches combined to send out a sufficient number of missionaries to bring about the evangelization of the entire world. It just cannot be done.

Now that does not mean that missionaries are not necessary. We must still send them out. They are the ones who, with the help of the native workers, will distribute the printed page. Without the missionaries we could not get out the message. Therefore we must still send out missionaries. But let us put the tools that they need in their hands. Let us give them the printed page. Churchill said: "Give us the tools and we will finish the job." Our missionaries are saying the same. If we can give them millions of copies of the Message, and they can systematically circulate it, then the world can be evangelized.

There are millions who will never be able to get the Gospel over the air. Therefore, important as radio is, it cannot do the job by itself. Bible Schools will continue to train nationals, but Bible Schools alone will not suffice. Mass evangelism, newspaper evangelism, loud speakers, transcriptions, and all the other methods, will continue to be used, but I do not believe that any of them will be able to reach "every creature".

I believe the Rev. Jack McAlister of World Literature Crusade has the secret. It is a long time since I have met a man with the missionary burden and passion that he has. He is clear in his thinking and he knows that the most effective method is the printed page. Therefore he is giving his life to the getting out of the message by means of literature, and he is reaching countless millions as a result.

We printed 100,000 copies of my little salvation booklet in the Portuguese language and distributed them in Portugal. They printed 300,000 in the Italian language in Rome and distributed them throughout Italy. We printed 50,000 copies in Spanish and distributed them throughout the Island of Cuba. We have gone to Korea, Formosa, France, and many other countries with our salvation booklets. Calls are coming in continually. We are getting the most amazing letters from those who read them, telling of wonderful conversions. Our missionaries are going to be kept busy on some fields taking care of the converts.

Remember, it only costs 14c., according to those who are doing the job, to win a soul to Jesus Christ by means of the printed page. That means that there is no cheaper way to carry on missionary work. If we can systematically put a copy of the printed page in every home in a given city, we will have reached "every creature" in that city, for we will have reached every member of the family. Our missionaries can organize a group of workers and send them from door to door, from house to house, with the message. That was Paul's method and therefore it is Scriptural. He evangelized from "house to house", so as to reach "every creature" with the Gospel message. We cannot do better than to follow his example. Let us take the printed page and place it in every home in our community and thus reach every soul for God.

As fast as the money comes in we are sending out the printed page, for we are simply deluged with requests. Our salvation booklets are now in some twenty-five different languages and we are putting them into more all the time. We have been doing this work for over thirty years, but today we are working at it as never before. We must have thousands upon thousands of dollars for the printed page if we are going to do the job that God wants us to do. No greater investment could possibly be made. We are sending out clear-cut Gospel messages that make the way of salvation perfectly clear and plain and we know that God is using them in a most amazing way. Miracles are happening wherever they are being distributed. But we must do much more. The fields are white unto harvest. Now is the time to garner in the sheaves.

I know of no method to compare with the printed page. It is needed on every field. The Bible says "The gospel must first be *published* among all nations" (Mark 13: 10). Well then, let us publish it. Let us put out simple salvation messages, filled with Scripture, and let us circulate them far and wide. Let us give them the Gospel by means of the printed page.

I am not suggesting that we distribute Bibles. The Old Testament will confuse the average reader, and its blood sacrifices are objectionable to such countries as India where animals are looked upon as sacred by most Hindus. Even the New Testament, if the reader starts with the chronology of Matthew, will be difficult. If you are going to give the Scriptures, giving the Gospel of John. But, if possible, John, Acts and Romans. Bibles should be given after conversion. I have never known anyone to be saved through the Old Testament alone. Even the Synoptic Gospels do not tell us how to be saved, but John, Acts and Romans do.

The eunuch, you remember, had the Word. Why, he was actually reading about Christ in Isaiah. Yet he could not see the light. A preacher had to explain it to him. So it is today. "How shall they hear without a preacher?" Even though they have the Bible? God's method is the sermon, the message. Eternal life, Jesus said, was not to be found in the Scriptures, but in Himself (John 5: 39–40).

And whether it is preached or read, it does the work.

That is, if it is a clear-cut salvation message. If it deals with the great salvation verses of the Bible. If it is based on the Scriptures. If it presents the Gospel and makes the way plain.

Bibles cost money. Brief salvation messages are inexpensive. In a booklet of sixteen pages, the Gospel can be clearly and forcefully presented and a soul won to Christ. Why then waste God's money? Why not put it where it will count most? Why not invest it in the printed page?

CHAPTER V

JUDGING OTHERS

YOU will find my text in Romans 11: 1. I am reading from the Phillips translation. "Now if you feel inclined to set yourself up as a judge of those who sin, let me assure you, whoever you are, that you are in no position to do so."

The awful sin of judging others has been creeping into the Church. That dreadful teaching, which has wrecked and ruined thousands all over the world and divided assemblies everywhere, which has resulted in broken friendships, broken fellowship, bitterness and heartache indescribable, seems to be Satan's most useful heresy for the wrecking of God's work and the putting of God's servants out of business. If he cannot strike from the outside he will strike from the inside.

It is all based on just one New Testament incident (1 Cor. 5), where an extreme case which had become a public scandal had to be dealt with. This man was *living* in sin; he would not give it up. It was not a single act. When a sin is known to everyone it has to be judged. But we must never forget that the same man who was excommunicated in 1 Corinthians 5 was forgiven and restored in 2 Corinthians 2: 1–11. We should do the same. Apart, I say, from this one and only incident, the whole of the teaching of the New Testament is absolutely against judging others. The emphasis is on forgiveness and restoration.

Judgment Forbidden

Let me again read my text. Listen! *"Now if you feel inclined to set yourself up as a judge of those who sin, let me assure you, whoever you are, that you are in no position to do so."* That should settle it. But in addition we have God's direct commandment. "And whensoever ye stand praying, forgive, if ye have aught against anyone; that your Father also which is in heaven may forgive you your trespasses" (Mark 11: 25–26). You see you are to forgive even when you are not asked to forgive, even when there is no repentance. You must not harbour a spirit of bitterness and unforgiveness in your heart. Strange, is it not, that those who judge and refuse to forgive, become bitter themselves? Their sin is greater in the sight of God than the sin of the one they condemn.

Those who judge never obey Galatians 6: 1, which is a definite command. They say they would be the first to forgive the offender *if* he showed signs of genuine repentance. But they never go to him to see if there are any such signs. They make no effort whatever to bring him to repentance and restoration. He is left entirely to himself. They refuse to obey Galatians 6: 1.

Self-Judgment

The New Testament has much to say about self-judgment; it has very little to say about judgment by others. It tells us to judge ourselves so that we might not be judged or chastened by God. "For if we would judge ourselves, we should not be judged. But when we are judged, we are chastened of the Lord" (1 Cor. 11: 31–32). I have preached all my life against the sins of the believer, but I never mention names. I never call him up on the carpet or before the Board. I urge him to judge himself, so that God will not have to judge him. In my books, especially *The Revival We Need,* I spend a lot of time exposing and condemning sin, but I leave God to apply the shoe to the one it fits. I know that a guilty conscience will condemn. I would never dream of setting myself up as a judge and taking things into my own hands. I do not even hint at judgment by others. I do not know all the facts and I never can, for I am finite. Only God is capable of righteous judgment. That is why He warns us to let Him do the judging and tells us not to judge others.

Proverbs does not teach Church truth, but Proverbs has a lot to say along this line. For instance, "Love covereth all sins" (10: 12); "He that uttereth a slander is a fool" (10: 18); "A talebearer revealeth secrets: but he that is of a faithful spirit concealeth the matter" (11: 13); "A whisperer separateth chief friends" (16: 28); "He that covereth a transgression seeketh love; but he that repeateth a matter separateth very friends" (17: 9); "The words of a talebearer are as wounds" (18: 8); "Where no wood is, there the fire goeth out; so where there is no talebearer, the strife ceaseth" (26: 20).

Examples of Judgment

Miriam, you will remember, was stricken with leprosy because she criticized and judged her brother Moses (Num. 12). Korah, Dathan and Abiram were swallowed up by an earthquake because they judged Moses and Aaron (Num. 16). "Whoso privily slandereth his neighbour, him will I cut off" (Ps. 101: 5).

In the early days of my ministry a certain woman started denouncing one of the officials of the Church. Our Board prayed and one night she choked to death. Later two church officers took it upon themselves to judge a couple of God's servants. One died and the other has lost his testimony and is out of the church. Still later, two other very active Christians sat in judgment on another, and they, too, lost their official positions and the fellowship of their brethren and are now out of active service. Still another, who was a great soul-winner, started criticizing and judging. Before long he backslid so fearfully that he gave up all church work and then ended up in transgression himself. There was one other, who was at one time deeply spiritual and enjoyed his work for God immensely, but he also began to judge his fellow Christians and, in a short time, he drifted away from the church, resigned his office and ended up in a most unhappy predicament. A married couple took it upon themselves to judge another. Today they are both out of the work entirely and their reputation for spirituality, and even honesty, is gone. Yet they were once leaders in the Lord's work.

So, you see, I have had plenty of experience in this matter of judging and I know exactly how it ends. It is a dangerous business. It is Satan's method of getting some of God's most useful servants out of the work. I refuse to allow the Church of God to become a police court.

Now some of those judged were guilty, but their accusers were not satisfied to let the Board or the Pastor deal with them. They, too, had to be the judges, and so they themselves were judged of God. I once heard of a church in which several of the officials set themselves up as judges. The committee in charge did all that they asked them to do, but so bitter had they become, that the leaders of the work gave themselves to prayer, asking God to lead them to send in their resignations. Months later they all suddenly resigned and thereby lost the fellowship of the entire church.

There are two kinds of sin, the sin of the flesh and the sin of the spirit. The prodigal son was guilty of the sin of the flesh and was forgiven. The elder brother was guilty of the sin of the spirit and was condemned. Jesus was always patient and forgiving with those who sinned in the flesh. His word was, "Neither do I condemn thee." He denounced in scathing words those who sinned in the spirit. The man who judges, like the elder brother, has no patience with the prodigal son.

God's Word

But what now does God's Word say about judging? Let us turn first of all to Matthew 7: 1–5, and we will read from the Phillips translation:

"Don't criticize people, and you will not be criticized. For you will be judged by the way you criticize others, and the measure you give will be the measure you get.

"Why do you look at the speck of sawdust in your brother's eye and fail to notice the plank in your own? How can you say to your brother, Let me get the speck out of your eye, when there is a plank in your own? You fraud! Take the plank out of your own eye first, and then you can see clearly enough to remove your brother's speck of dust."

Now let us study Romans 14: 10, 13, and again I quote from the Phillips translation:

"Why, then, criticize your brother's actions, why try to make him look small? We shall all be judged one day, not by each other's standards or even our own, but by the standards of Christ. Let us therefore stop turning critical eyes on one another. If we must be critical, let us be critical of our own conduct and see that we do nothing to make a brother stumble or fall."

Church Discipline

But what about Church Discipline, you ask? That, too, is dealt with in God's Word. First of all, however, remember Hebrews 13: 17. "Obey them that have the rule over you." Your pastor has been placed over you in the Lord. It is up to you to obey him. Let him decide what to do. Once you have reported the matter to him, your responsibility ceases, even if you are an official of the church. It is now up to him and you must abide by his decision.

The method of procedure is clearly outlined in Matthew 18: 15–17. First he will deal with the offender personally with the hope of settling the trouble. If he fails, he will choose one or two others, as directed in Matthew, and try again. Then, as a last resort—and only as a last resort— he will call a meeting of the Board or the members of the church. If that, too, fails, he will have no choice but to exercise discipline.

Let me say that I have followed this procedure for nearly half-a-century and only once have I had to call in the officials of the church. To call a meeting of the Board to deal with personal accusations would be the last thing I would do. That is not God's method and it never works. The Pharisee and the Legalist will expose and condemn. The Christian will cover up and restore (Prov. 17: 9).

"Now I beseech you, brethren, *mark them which cause divisions and offences* contrary to the doctrine which you have learned; and avoid them. For they that are such serve not our Lord Jesus Christ, but their own belly; and by good words and fair speeches deceive the hearts of the simple" (Rom. 16: 17–18). Nothing will cause divisions and offences like judging others. Therefore do not do it. And keep away from those who do. "Who art thou that judgest another" (Rom. 14: 4). Leave all judgment to the Judgment Seat of Christ.

CHAPTER VI

VICTORY THROUGH CHRIST

YOU will find my text in 1 Corinthians 15: 57: "Thanks be to God, which giveth us the victory through our Lord Jesus Christ."

The saddest experience in the Christian life is the presence and power of sin. To be on the mountain top today and down in the valley tomorrow, to be in the eighth chapter of Romans today and back in the seventh chapter tomorrow, to be in the Promised Land today and then back in the wilderness again tomorrow, to be up today and down tomorrow—that, I say, is the saddest experience that I know anything about.

God has said in unmistakable words, "Sin shall not have dominion over you." When Paul comes to the end of that terrible seventh chapter of Romans and cries out in the anguish of his soul, "O wretched man that I am! who shall deliver me?" the answer comes as though spoken by a voice from Heaven: "I thank God . . . Jesus Christ our Lord." So then victory is possible. Victory is within the reach of every one of us. "Sin shall not have dominion over you."

Two Classes of Sins

Now, there are only two classes of sins known to humanity. First of all there are what we call "outward" sins, and then "inward" sins. By outward sins I mean the sins with which we are all more or less familiar, sins such as murder, drunkenness, blasphemy, etc. I am not talking about outward sin. If you have been saved at all, then you have already been delivered from outward sin. If not, then there is no evidence that you have ever passed out of death and into life. But I am talking about inward sins. When I refer to inward sins I am referring to some sins that the average Christian does not even designate as sin at all. I am referring to such sins as worry and anxiety, unforgiveness and hatred, grudge-bearing, malice, wrath, anger, jealousy and pride. I am referring to such sins as impurity and uncleanness, secret sins, sins that the eye of man cannot see. I am thinking of a host of other sins that are continually rising up and clamouring for recognition. These, I say, are the sins of the Christian and the sins from which he must obtain deliverance.

My friend, you have a besetting sin. I have a besetting sin. You will probably overcome most of the sins to which you have been addicted. But there will be one besetting sin that will dog your footsteps wherever you go. It is with that sin that you will have to deal. You know what it is and God knows what it is. It may be anger. Perhaps you lose your temper and fly off the handle. It may be impurity, some secret sin. It may be hatred or unforgiveness. I say *you* know what it is. I do not. It is that sin you will have to deal with if you are going to be a victorious Christian. You will never know happiness until you have been delivered. As long as you yield to your besetting sin you will be miserable. To be continually sinning and repenting, I say, is one of the most miserable experiences that I know anything about.

As long as you are yielding to sin, God cannot use you. "If I regard iniquity in my heart, the Lord will not hear me." He will not even bend down and listen to what you say, let alone use you in His service. You will never know what it is to be a happy Christian. Before you can enjoy God's salvation you will have to be victorious over sin. It is the little foxes that spoil the vines. These are the sins, I say, to which Christians are addicted. Do you know the secret of deliverance? Have you been able to overcome your besetting sin?

Sinless Perfection and Suppression

Now I am not talking about sinless perfection. I am making no reference whatever to eradication or suppression. These words are not found in the Bible, therefore

I do not use them. As a matter of fact I am not even interested in the doctrine. I would a thousand times rather be wrong in my head and right in my heart, than to be right in my head and wrong in my heart. I would rather have the theory wrong and the practice right, than to have the theory right and the practice wrong. I want an outcome. I want to know that I am a victorious Christian.

Whenever I think of suppression I think of a story of an old Quaker woman and a new convert. They were standing side by side. Presently a terrible provocation crossed the pathway of the old Quaker woman. But during the entire time of the provocation she continued smiling just as sweetly as she had been smiling before. After it was all over the young Christian turned to her. "Say," she said, "I can't understand how you could keep your temper under a provocation such as that." The old Quaker woman, still smiling, and thinking she knew the secret of victory, turned to the younger Christian and this was her answer: "Ah, thee didn't see the boiling inside." You see, she really thought she was victorious, yet all the time she was boiling furiously on the inside; she was as angry as she could be. But she kept smiling so that the younger Christian would not know it.

My friend, if it's boiling, it's boiling. If it's there, it's there. So far as men are concerned, if you can keep it on the inside, well and good; but so far as God is concerned, you might as well explode and be through with it altogether, for if it's there, I say, it's there. It doesn't matter whether you boil on the inside or the outside, if you're boiling, you're boiling. God can see it. And, whether you boil on the inside or on the outside, you have lost the victory; even though you manage to hide it from the eyes of others.

I think of another story. Two boys were wrestling. One was a big boy, the other was a little boy. After a while, to the amazement of everyone, the little fellow got the big fellow down. But as soon as he got him down he got astride him and just sat there. Those standing by wondered why he did not get up and let him go. After a while a young man came along. "Say, young fellow," he said, "you've won the wrestling match, why are you sitting there? Why don't you get up and let him go?" The little fellow looked up with a grin on his face and this was his answer: "Ah," he said, "I can feel him arisin', sir." And he knew very well that if he arose, he might be underneath and the big fellow might be on top. So he thought he'd better sit tight and hold what he had, while he had what he had. "I can feel him arisin', sir." Have you ever felt him "arisin'"? Or am I talking some kind of a strange dialect that you can't understand?

You know what I mean. Just when you are having a lovely party; you have invited some Christian people to your home and you want to make a good impression. Suddenly someone steps on your toe. Someone says something behind your back. Somebody criticizes you and, before you realize it, you are conscious of a rising inside, and, sooner or later, you fly off the handle and everyone knows that you lost your temper. And, before anyone will believe in your testimony again, you will have to go back to the altar and get right with God.

You know, it is a terrible thing to have to sit on a safety-valve all your life. Safety-valves have a habit of blowing off at unexpected moments. I am so glad I've found One who can take care of the safety-valve for me, while I go and do His work. My friend, Jesus Christ can deliver you from the boiling inside, from the rising within. You do not have to lose your temper. You do not have to fly off the handle. You can be a victorious Christian.

Dr. A. B. Simpson, the great founder of the Christian and Missionary Alliance, expressed it this way: "Everything in Jesus and Jesus Everything." That little couplet went around the world. Thousands upon thousands who had been trying to be victorious by believing a doctrine, realized at last that victory was in a Person, not in a doctrine, and they stepped out of defeat into glorious blood-bought victory. Other thousands, who believed that victory was in an experience, also came to realize that victory was in a Person, and they, too, stepped out of defeat into victory. They came to realize that victory was through another, and that "other" was the Lord Jesus Christ.

Old Testament Examples

Away back in the Old Testament you have it stated very clearly: "Ye shall not need to fight in this battle." This is the way it reads: "Stand ye still, and see the salvation of the Lord, which he will work for you this day, for the battle is not yours, but God's." Did you ever hear of that kind of a battle? A battle in which you stand still? You see, God is to do the work for you. The battle is not yours, it is His. Oh, if I could only get everyone to go out, saying, with each step, "The battle is not mine, the battle is not mine, the battle is the Lord's, the battle is the Lord's," it would spell the difference between defeat and victory. This is not your battle, my friend; it is God's battle. Jesus is to become your Victor, and only when He does will you know the secret of the Victorious Life.

Do you remember when Joshua went to view the walls of Jericho? He saw a man standing over against the walls and he challenged him. "Art thou for us or for our adversaries?" What did the man say? "Nay," he said, "but as captain of the Lord's host am I now come." What did Joshua say? Did he say, "Well, captain, I'm glad to see you, but I don't need your help. I have a great army. Jericho is a very small city. We can capture it without your assistance?" Had he said that, Jericho might never have fallen. What did he say? "What saith my Lord unto his servant?" Do you remember what happened on that never-to-be-forgotten day? The Lord's host, those mighty, invisible angels of God, were placed on the battlements of the walls and, after the people had marched around and when they shouted, the captain of the Lord's host gave the word of command and, with one mighty shove, those angels overthrew the walls of Jericho and they fell down flat.

My friends, the Captain of the Lord's hosts is here right now. He is going from heart to heart and from life to life.

He is saying, "You have failed in the past. You have lost your temper again and again. You have sinned time after time. That besetting sin of yours has overcome you. You have never been able to conquer it. Now let Me undertake for you. Let Me fight your battle. Let Me overcome your enemy. Let Me be your Victor. I'll defeat your foe, and then I'll come back and give you the credit for the victory." Wouldn't that be wonderful? That, my friends, is exactly what He wants to do, and you must let Him. He must fight your battles.

Illustrations

Here is a man who is drowning. He goes down for the first time, struggling furiously. A man stands on the bank with folded arms, but makes no effort to rescue him. Again, for the second time, he goes down, still struggling as furiously as ever. Still the man stands on the bank, yet makes no move to save him. Now he is going down for the third and last time. But he doesn't struggle any more. He realizes that it is useless. Allowing his arms to fall by his sides, he cries out in a feeble voice, "Help!" and, in a moment, the man standing on the bank unfolds his arms, dives in, and easily rescues the drowning man.

Why didn't he do it before? Because he thought he could effect his own rescue, he thought he could save himself. He had to be left to struggle until he realized that it was all up; that it was no use, and that he was going to drown. Then, when he gave up, he was ready to let someone else undertake. The rescuer could dive in and save him.

My friend, the reason you are not victorious is because you are too strong. You have too much will power. You think you can save yourself. You have an idea you can effect your own rescue, that you do not need outside help. Never will you be victorious until you admit your weakness, your helplessness, until you turn to someone else, and let Him deliver you.

Here is a little girl who has been recently saved. "Little girl," asks her teacher, "where is Jesus now?" She thinks

c

for a moment and then, as she looks up into her teacher's face, with a bright smile, she answers. "Teacher," she says, "Jesus is in my heart." "Yes," says the teacher, "Jesus is in your heart. Now, little girl, what will you do tomorrow if Satan comes and knocks at the door of your heart?" Again she thinks. Finally she gives an answer that very few mature Christians would think of giving. "Teacher," she says, "I'd send Jesus to the door."

Now, my friends, suppose you fail to grasp the secret of victory. Tomorrow Satan comes and knocks at the door of your heart. It is your old temptation, your besetting sin. Quickly you hurry to the door. Satan stoops down and looks through the key-hole and, as he sees you coming, he grins to himself. Many a time he has conquered you in the past and he knows he can conquer you again. You do not throw the door wide open. No one ever sins like that. You just open it a little way, so that you can talk to Satan through the crack. You turn your temptation over as a sweet morsel. You meditate on it. Presently, before you realize what has happened, he puts his foot in the crack. Then, edging around and around, at last he is on the inside, and, once again, you have gone down in defeat. You have failed.

Now, suppose you *do* grasp the secret of victory. Again Satan comes and knocks at the door of your heart. "Jesus! Jesus" you exclaim. "Yes, my child, what is it?" "Jesus, that's Satan, that's my old besetting sin." "Yes, my child, I know," answers Jesus. "What do you want Me to do?" "Jesus, will you go to the door? Will You answer Satan?" "Yes, my child, you just sit here and trust Me. I'll go and deal with your temptation."

Jesus goes to the door. Again Satan stoops down and looks through the key-hole. This time he sees, coming toward him, the Son of God. He knows that Jesus has often defeated him before and that He can defeat him again. Jesus throws the door wide open and steps out on the porch. I doubt if He will see Satan for dust down the street. Quietly He returns. "My child," He says, "you

have won the victory." "*I* have won the victory, Lord?
What do you mean? *You* have won the victory." "No,
my child, you have won the victory." "But, Lord, I have
not done anything. I have just been sitting here trusting
You. *You've* won the victory." "Yes, my child. That is
the way you and I are going to fight your battles in the
days to come. You are going to sit still and trust. I am
going to go out and do the fighting. Then I'll come back
and give you the credit for the victory. Thus you will
always be victorious."

My friends, isn't that a wonderful way to fight? Isn't
it wonderful to have someone else to do your fighting for
you? You know, you do not get hurt when someone else
fights your battles. I was delicate when I was a boy. I
was not big and robust and strong, like I am now. I never
could do my own fighting. Whenever I had a fight on my
hands I always had to go and find a bigger boy and ask
him to do my fighting for me. Then all I had to do was
to stand still and watch. I was never defeated. I never
got hurt. I always won the victory. That, I say, is a
wonderful way to fight. But so few of us are willing to
fight like that. Most of us want to do our own fighting.
We are not ready to let someone else do our fighting for
us. Thus we go down continually in defeat.

Paul Rader

Many of you know, or have heard about, the great
American evangelist, Paul Rader. I knew him very, very
well indeed. Many a time he called me on the telephone
and asked me to go to Chicago to preach in his great
tabernacle, when he was going to be away holding a
campaign somewhere. Time after time I have faced his
audience of some three thousand people and I have seen
the altar full, as men and women responded to the invitation. Many times I invited him to Toronto to preach for
me. I say, I knew him very well.

But not only was Paul Rader a great evangelist, he was
also a great pugilist. As a matter of fact he fought thirty-
three battles in the ring and was never once knocked out.

He weighed some 240 pounds and he always came off victor.

One day I was spending an evening with him, when my curiosity got the better of me. "Mr. Rader," I said, "will you let me feel your muscle?" He looked at me somewhat perplexed and then, standing to his feet, he took off his coat, rolled up his sleeve, folded his arm and, turning to me, said: "Put it there." I felt those great steel muscles of his, and, even as I talk about it now, I can still feel them.

Now, suppose he had said to me: "My friend, I want to challenge you to a fight in the ring." Suppose I had answered, "All right, Mr. Rader, I'll be very glad to take you on." But, even while saying it, I would know perfectly well he would never have to strike me. He would just pat me gently and I would lie down unconscious. He would just tap me a little bit and I would see stars. Nevertheless, I accept his challenge.

Immediately I find my way to Jack Dempsey. "Mr. Dempsey," I say, "I have a fight on my hands, a fight with Paul Rader, the man who has never been knocked out, and who may some day become the heavyweight champion of the world. Would you be willing to take this fight off my hands? Would you be willing to meet Paul Rader on my behalf?" Mr. Dempsey answers, "Why, certainly. I'll be delighted to take the fight off your hands. I'll be very glad to meet your opponent in the ring."

Well, the great night of the fight comes. I take my seat somewhere outside the ropes in an easy chair. I never have been at one of those affairs and I never expect to be, but I know I would be outside the ropes. Presently I see the huge form of Mr. Radar coming through the curtains in the farther corner, and, as I look at his great steel muscles, I am very glad that I am not inside the ropes. Then I look in the other direction and I see Mr. Dempsey coming out. Of course no one there knows that the other man is Mr. Dempsey. Everyone thinks that Paul Rader's opponent is Oswald J. Smith. The referee gives his instructions and the fight starts.

Suddenly, to the amazement of everyone, Mr. Dempsey strikes the decisive blow and, for the first time in his life, Paul Rader goes down and is counted out. Then the referee lifts the arm of the other and calls out to the gathered thousands, "Oswald J. Smith has won." Then newspaper headlines all over the world, and, in the American papers, headlines nearly a foot deep, appear with the announcement, "New Heavyweight Champion— Oswald J. Smith, Heavyweight Champion of the World!" I haven't struck a blow and yet I'm heavyweight champion of the world.

Do you see what I mean? You know, it is wonderful to fight like that. As I said before, you never get hurt and you always win. But there are so few who are willing to let others do their fighting.

Listen, my friend, I would be a fool to go into the ring with Paul Rader, for I wouldn't stand a chance. But you are a greater fool when you go into the ring with Satan, for you haven't a ghost of a chance. Satan has been on the job for over six thousand years. He knows your weakest point. He knows exactly how to defeat you, and yet you think you can match yourself against him. You haven't sense enough to let someone else do your fighting for you. What should you do? You should do exactly what I would do, if Paul Rader were to challenge me. You should go and find someone bigger and stronger. And the only One I know, who is stronger than Satan, is the Lord Jesus Christ. When you are challenged you should go to Him and ask Him to fight for you. He can defeat Satan. He knows how to do it. You can be victorious as He fights your battles.

Can Such a Life be Lived?

Can such a life be lived? Let me put it this way: Has Jesus Christ ever kept you in victory for a minute? You say He has. Well, then, if He can keep you victorious for a minute, why not for a week, a month, or a year? It takes just the same current to drive the street-car one mile as it does to drive it ten miles. You are not a storage battery. God does not wind you up and leave you to yourself. You are in contact with a live wire and, as long as you are, there is victory. As soon as the contact has been broken, there is defeat.

As long as Peter kept his eyes on Jesus, he walked on the water. As soon as he got his eyes off Jesus, he commenced to sink. When he got his eyes back on Jesus again, he walked once more. As long as the iron is in the fire, the fire is in the iron. As soon as you take the iron out of the fire, the fire comes out of the iron. As long as you are in contact with Jesus Christ, you are victorious.

Major Whittle one time read that hymn: "I Need Thee Every Hour." "That will never do," he said. "I need Him every moment." Right there and then he sat down and wrote "Moment by moment I'm kept in His love, Moment by moment I've life from above; Looking to Jesus till glory doth shine, Moment by moment, O Lord, I am Thine." In other words, it is a moment by moment experience. And only as you walk with God, only as you keep in touch with the Lord Jesus Christ, moment by moment, day by day, will you be a victorious Christian. There is no experience that you can get at an altar that will last you for a lifetime. Thousands of Christians have spent countless hours at altars pleading for victory. There is no easy way. Victory is the result of a walk, a constant walk with God. Only those who are in daily touch with the Lord Jesus Christ are victorious.

How To Do It

I want you, now, to get alone with God, to go over all your sins of the past, to make a full and complete confession, because He says that "If we confess our sins, he is faithful and just to forgive us our sins." Sin confessed is sin forgiven. Sin forgiven is sin cleansed. After you have confessed your sins, plead the cleansing blood. Make sure that every sin has been confessed, especially your besetting sin, and trust God to forgive you and to cleanse you in the blood. Name your sins. Be definite. Take time about it. Don't be in a hurry. Drag them all out, every Achan in the camp, and make certain that there are no reservations.

Then, after there has been a full and complete confession, after you have been cleansed and forgiven, then dare to take Jesus Christ as your Victor. Now, listen. Years ago, perchance, you took Him as your Saviour. That was a very definite experience. This experience must be just as definite. You must open your heart to Jesus Christ and receive Him as your Victor, just as you once received Him as your Saviour.

Not only did the children of Israel cross the Red Sea; they also crossed the Jordan River. You may have crossed the Red Sea. You may have been converted, but have you crossed the Jordan River? Have you accepted Jesus Christ as your Victor? Are you able to say, "Jesus is Victor"? Has there been a definite transaction, a definite crisis experience? Or have you never yet known such an experience?

My friend, you may grow in grace, and you will, but there must be a starting point. You get nothing until you start. There is a beginning to everything. There must be a beginning to victory. There must be a moment when you step out of defeat into victory. When you turn from the old life to the new. When you leave the Wilderness for the Promised Land. When you cross the Jordan River. I say, there must be a definite crisis experience. There must be a start. Have you ever started? You can't get anywhere till you start. If you have never started, then, if I were you, I would start at once. I would have a definite crisis experience with the Lord Jesus Christ. I would take Him as my Victor, just as I once took Him as my Saviour. I would be definite about it.

What if you fail?

Now let me say something very, very important. You will go out expecting to live a victorious life, but you will fail again, and then you will be discouraged and you will say: "It doesn't work. It's no use. I cannot be a victorious Christian." My friend, listen. Did you ever see a little baby trying to learn to walk? I have. What happens? Well, the little baby tumbles. Then what? Does it just lie down on the floor on its back and say, "Well, it's no use. I see other people walking around me, but I'll never be able to learn to walk. I have had a tumble. I've fallen. I can't walk"? No, never. Never have you heard a baby talk like that. What does the baby do? It tumbles. It has a good cry. Then it immediately gets up and it starts to walk again. It may have another tumble. Perhaps half a dozen. But, finally, it will find itself walking and there will be no more tumbling. Its days of tumbling will be over.

Now, why did it tumble? Why did it fall? Because its little legs were weak. They had to become strong. So it is with you, my friend. Your spiritual legs are weak. You haven't walked in victory for years. Don't be surprised, then, if you have a few tumbles at the beginning. As you are learning to walk in victory you may tumble again and again. Don't get discouraged. Don't go back on what you have done. You have claimed Jesus as your Victor. You took Him as your Victor. Now praise Him and tell Him that He is still your Victor, even though you have tumbled, even though you have fallen, even though you have again yielded to your besetting sin. Get up. Have a good cry. Confess your failure to God. Ask Him to forgive you. Tell Him you never meant to fail. Tell Him you want to be victorious. Then start again. Walk once more. Proclaim Jesus as your Victor as before.

What will happen? Presently, to your amazement, you will discover that you are not having any more falls. You are not tumbling. Your old besetting sin has lost its hold on you. You have been delivered. You have been set free. You are now walking. You are in daily contact with Jesus Christ. Moment by moment you are looking to Him, relying upon Him, letting Him fight your battles, letting Him win the victory for you. Instead of defeat, there is victory. You are now a victorious Christian because Jesus is living His life out from within.

You Cannot Live the Christian Life

Remember, you have never lived the Christian life and you never can live the Christian life. No one ever has. No one ever will. The only One who has ever lived the Christian life is the Lord Jesus Christ. He was the perfect man, as well as the Son of God. What, then, is the Christian life? The Christian life is the outliving of the indwelling Christ. As He indwells in the power of the Holy Spirit, He lives out His life from within. People see the Christian life being lived. You know you are not living it. You realize that Jesus Christ is living it in you and through you. You cannot live it, but He can. So you just let go and let God. That, my friends, is the Christian life. In other words, that is the Victorious Life. Jesus is Victor. He indwells and He lives out, through you, His own victorious life.

I've seen thousands upon thousands of orange trees. Never yet have I heard an orange tree say, "I am so afraid I may bear crab-apples instead of oranges." I have never known an orange tree to lament and cry and stand there in fear and trembling for fear it might make a mistake. What does it do? It just stands still. It just automatically produces oranges. It never once makes a mistake and produces crab-apples. Why? Because in its branches is the juice of the orange. What is in comes out. The sap within reproduces itself in the form of oranges without any effort on the part of the tree itself. So it is with you. If Jesus Christ indwells in His glorious fulness, the result will be a Victorious Life, for He will live out His life from within. It will require no effort on your part. All you have to do is to keep in contact with Him.

"Thanks be unto God which giveth us the victory." How? Through our efforts, our struggles, our endeavours? No. "Through the Lord Jesus Christ." Victory through another. Victory through Christ. It is a gift. You cannot earn it. You cannot merit it. He gives it. It is not through your efforts, or your endeavours, or your struggles. It is through Him, through the Lord Jesus Christ. There is no other way of victory. If you want to be a victorious Christian, you will have to receive Him as your Victor, let Him indwell you, keep in constant contact with Him by prayer and Bible study, and then, as you walk with Him, He will manifest Himself through you, and that will be the Victorious Life. It is victory through Christ. There is no other way.

This, my friends, is the easiest life that can be lived. The life of the back-slider is hard. Life in the wilderness is difficult. A life of victory and defeat by turns is most unsatisfactory. The only happy life, the only easy life, the only natural life, is the Victorious Life. Oh, the joy of Victory through Christ!

CHAPTER VII

WHAT HAPPENS WHEN A CHRISTIAN SINS?

WHAT happens when a Christian sins? Is he lost and lost forever? Does God cast him out, or is he still God's Child? If so, how does God deal with him? There are six things that I want to say in answering this question:

1. *The Christian does not practise sin*

He practises righteousness. He lives a righteous life. In 1 John 3: 6, 8 and 9, we find these words: "Whosoever abideth in him sinneth not: whosoever sinneth hath not seen him, neither known him. He that committeth sin is of the devil; Whosoever is born of God does not commit sin; for his seed remaineth in him: and he cannot sin, because he is born of God. In this the children of God are manifest, and the children of the devil."

The words in these verses are in the present progressive tense. The words used are "sinneth not" or "committeth sin". The child of God does not practise sin. He does not live in sin. He does not continue to indulge in sin. The practice of sin does not characterize his life. In other words, he does not keep sinning. If he does, then it is evident that he is not born of God. He still belongs to Satan.

2. *But he may fall into sin*

"My little children, these things write I unto you, that ye sin not. And if any man sin, we have an advocate with the Father, Jesus Christ the righteous: And he is the propitiation for our sins" (1 John 2: 1–2). It is clear, then, that the Christian does not have to sin. It is not necessary for him to commit known or deliberate sin. He can be set free from sin and he need not fall into sin. "These things write I unto you, that ye sin not."

On the other hand, provision is made for the Christian who does sin. God says: "If any man sin," clearly indicating that a Christian *may* sin. He may fall into sin, even though it is not his normal life. He is like the needle of a compass. The needle always points to the north, but it is possible for something to detract it and, for a moment, it may point in another direction, but inevitably it will swing back and point again north. So it is with the Christian. He does not practise sin, he does not need to sin. On the other hand, he may fall into sin. If he does, he has an advocate, the Lord Jesus Christ. He becomes a mercy-seat, a propitiation. His sin can be forgiven.

It is like the sheep and the sow. Here is a mud puddle, for instance. The sheep gets too near and suddenly falls in. The sow does not have to fall in. The moment it sees the mud puddle it makes a bee-line straight for it and wades in of its own free will. But now what happens? The sheep immediately scrambles out, and, when it gets out, it gets as far away from the mud puddle as possible. It does not remain in the mire. The sow, on the other hand, stays in the mud puddle. It makes no effort to get out. It is now in its natural environment. It loves the mire.

So it is with the believer. He is like the sheep. He may fall in unexpectedly, but he immediately scrambles out. He confesses his sin and turns back to God. He wants to be cleansed in the precious blood. When he gets out, he immediately gets away from the mud puddle. The sheep acts like that because it is a sheep.

The unsaved man, like the sow, wallows in the mire. He loves it. It is his natural element. He seeks it and settles down in it. He stays in the mire of sin. The sow stays in the mire because it is a sow. That is its nature. So it is with the sinner. Thus you can tell a sheep from a sow, and thus you can tell God's child from Satan's child. Both may fall in, but only one stays in. The Christian does not practise sin. He does not remain in the mud puddle. The sow does, and so does the sinner. It is not because you "fall in" that you are proved an unbeliever. It is because you stay in. Both may fall in, but only one stays in. The sinner practises sin. He lives in sin. He delights in sin. The Christian, on the other hand, detests his sin and turns from it, even though in his weakness he may yield to it.

3. *If he sins God will not disinherit him and cast him out*

He says in John 6: 37: "Him that cometh to me I will in no wise cast out." God will never disinherit him. He will deal with him as with a son. Now, how does a father deal with a son? Well, let us see what God has to say about it. Suppose we turn to Psalm 89 and read from verse 30 to verse 34: "If his children forsake my law, and walk not in my judgments; if they break my statutes, and keep not my commandments; then will I visit their transgression with the rod, and their iniquity with stripes. Nevertheless my loving-kindness will I not utterly take from him, nor suffer my faithfulness to fail. My covenant will I not break, nor alter the thing that is gone out of my lips."

What will God do if His children forsake His law and walk not in His judgments? If they break His statutes and keep not His commandments? Will He break His covenant with them? Will He alter the thing that has gone out of His lips? By no means. God says He will chastise them. He will punish them. He will visit their transgression with the rod and their iniquity with stripes. He will never take His loving kindness away from them. His faithfulness will never fail. But He will judge them just as a father judges his children.

What does a father do when his children disobey? He chastises them, does he not? They have to bear their punishment, and the punishment is for the purpose of correction. He wants to win them back, and so he applies the rod. God will do the same. The punishment may be severe, very severe. When God chastises, there is suffering. But just as a father chastises and punishes, just as a father gives a thrashing when needed, so God will chastise His children. No father would show his son the door and tell him to get out and never come back. He is still his child. He is still in the family. Therefore, he corrects him by means of chastisement. God does the same.

You have the same truth set forth in 2 Samuel 7: 13–15: "I will be his father, and he shall be my son. If he commit iniquity, I will chasten him with the rod of men, and with the stripes of the children of men: but my mercy shall not depart away from him."

Thus, you see, God is our Father and we are His children. When we commit iniquity He chastises us. He uses the rod. We have to bear the stripes. But, while He punishes us, He does not take away His mercy from us. We are still His children. We are still in the family, and He deals with us as members of His family.

4. *Fellowship has been broken, but confession restores it*

Now, in 1 John 1: 9, we read these words: "If we confess our sins, he is faithful and just to forgive us our sins, and to cleanse us from all unrighteousness." The moment we sin, fellowship is broken. We are no longer in communion. Sin has come between. When a child disobeys his father, he is no longer in fellowship with his father, and if he wants the fellowship restored, he must confess his disobedience and ask forgiveness. Then, and only then, is reconciliation possible.

Many of God's children, I fear, are out of fellowship with Him. They have no joy and no peace, simply because they are living in disobedience. They are not doing the things that God wants them to do. They have failed Him. They have sinned against Him. They have transgressed. He is waiting for them to confess their failure and get right so that they may be restored. As long as fellowship is broken prayer cannot be answered. Nothing but confession, restitution and forgiveness can restore it. But the moment we confess our sin He forgives us. "And the blood of Jesus Christ his Son cleanseth us from all sin"

(1 John 1: 7). It is not the sinner, remember, who is told to confess his sins. All he has to do is to confess that he is a sinner, just as the publican did when he cried out: "God be merciful to me a sinner." It is the Christian who must confess his sins.

You see, he has got off the road. He must get back on again. The only way he can get on is by admitting his mistake and returning. If two are walking together and one wanders off, their fellowship has been interrupted. The one who has wandered away will have to come back, if the fellowship is to be renewed. That may be the reason why you are so unhappy. You are out of fellowship with God. You are His child, but communion has been interrupted. Fellowship has been broken.

5. *Thus the Christian judges himself. If he doesn't, he will be judged of God*

Look now, if you will, at 1 Corinthians 11: 27–32: "Wherefore whosoever shall eat this bread, and drink this cup of the Lord, unworthily, shall be guilty of the body and blood of the Lord. But let a man examine himself, and so let him eat of that bread, and drink of that cup. For he that eateth and drinketh unworthily, eateth and drinketh damnation to himself, not discerning the Lord's body. For this cause many are weak and sickly among you, and many sleep. For if we would judge ourselves, we should not be judged. But when we are judged, we are chastened of the Lord, that we should not be condemned with the world."

Now, to eat unworthily means to eat without having confessed the sin of which the believer has been guilty. It must be confessed and put away. There must be cleansing and forgiveness before partaking of the Communion. God tells the believer to examine himself. In other words, to judge himself. Then He says that, if he doesn't, he eats and drinks damnation to himself. However, the word is not damnation but judgment. In other words, he will be chastised.

Now that is why God says that many of His children

are weak and sickly. Some, He states, have even died. I do not say that all sickness is caused by sin. Far from it. But it is possible for weakness and sickness to be the result of unconfessed sin. That may be why you have lost your job. God is dealing with you. He is judging you. You are being chastised. He wants you to be brought back into fellowship and communion once again. If He sees that you will not confess your sin, and that you are still going to dishonour Him and put Him to shame, then He may even take your life. If He does, you will have to face your transgressions at the Bema, or the Judgment Seat of Christ, and there, perchance, suffer the loss of all things. He must either judge you now or then.

Now He tells us that if we will judge ourselves we shall not be judged. In other words, if we will recognize our sin and confess it and be forgiven, then God will not have to chastise us. The only way you can escape chastisement is by judging yourself. Unless you make the wrong right God will have to deal with you. If you will judge yourself, then He will not have to judge you. There is no other way to escape chastisement except by immediately confessing your sin, being forgiven, and getting right with God. If a child were to do that the father would not punish him, but if the child refuses to get right then the father has to chastise. So it is with God.

Now God says very clearly that when He judges us He chastises us. That is the nature of God's judgment. And the reason He chastises us is because we are His children and He does not want to condemn us with the world. He wants us to be saved. But if we are His children, then He is going to deal with us as children. Thus we have to endure the chastisement of God. That may be why you are suffering right now. God is judging you, God is chastising you, and the only way you can get rid of God's chastisement is by confessing your sin and getting right with Him.

6. *Walking in the light procures daily cleansing*

In I John I: 7 we read, "But if we walk in the light, as he is in the light, we have fellowship one with another, and the blood of Jesus Christ his Son cleanseth us from all sin." We walk in the light by obeying God, by turning from everything we know to be wrong and living in the centre of God's will. When we turn to sin we are not walking in the light, because we know that sin is wrong. Now the man who walks in the light is cleansed daily from his sin.

I used to think that I had to ask God to forgive me for the last sin I had committed in order to be saved. Then I discovered one day that God has made provision for daily cleansing. As a matter of fact, as I walk in the light and live for God I am cleansed day and night, whether awake or asleep. The blood of Jesus Christ is continually cleansing me from all sin, so that I am always ready to meet God.

Jesus, you remember, wanted to wash Peter's feet. Peter refused, and Jesus told him that unless He washed his feet he could have no part with Him. Peter then wanted to be washed all over. In other words, he wanted a complete bath. But Jesus told him that if he had been washed once, if he had had a bath—in other words, if he had been converted, if he had been saved—he did not need to be washed over again. He did not need another complete bath. But his feet were being defiled as they came into contact with the dust of the road, moment by moment, and, therefore, they had to be cleansed, and so Jesus insisted on washing Peter's feet.

Now, my friend, you have been saved, you have had a complete bath, you have been born again, you are now God's child. But you are in daily contact with the world, and as long as you are—as long as you are in your body —there will be defilement, there will be stains—whether you see them or not—and you will need constant cleansing. God has made provision for you. The blood of Jesus Christ His Son continually cleanses you from all sin. That

D

is, if you walk in the light. If you do the things that you know to be right, and abstain from the things that you know to be wrong.

May I beseech you, therefore, to turn to God the moment you sin. You ought not to sin, but you may sin. If you do, you will repent immediately, if you are God's child, and you will ask to be forgiven. Fellowship has been broken, communion interrupted. But now, by confessing your sin and being cleansed in the blood, you are restored, and once again you are in fellowship and communion with the Lord Jesus Christ. You have now judged yourself. God will not have to judge you. If you refuse to judge yourself, then you will have to face the judgment of God. If, on the other hand, you walk in the light, the blood of Jesus Christ will cleanse you continuously from all sin.

That is what happens when a Christian sins. I am so glad that God has made ample provision, that He has recognized the possibility of sin, and that, instead of casting us out and disinheriting us when we fail Him, He deals with us as children, as members of His family. We can be forgiven and restored, and, once again, we can walk with God. Only then will His joy be ours. Only then will His peace abide in our hearts. Only then will we be in fellowship with one another and with the Lord Jesus Christ.

CHAPTER VIII

TRAINING FOR SERVICE

THERE are two kinds of Christian workers, those who have taken the prescribed course of training and those who have not. This course, with most denominations, consists of four years of high school, three or four years of college and three years of seminary.

But what about those who have been converted too late in life and are now too old to go back to school and take the course? What about those who, because of physical infirmity or financial responsibilities, have been unable to complete high school or to attend college? Are they to be denied?

That is why Bible schools like Nyack and Moody were born. They recognized that the church was losing some of its finest workers just because of its scholastic standards. Hence, they invited those who did not have the necessary qualifications, to become students. They provided a first-class Bible course along with as much practical training as possible, and then sent them out as missionaries, pastors and evangelists, and they made good. Had the denominations recognized their value, they too would have made some kind of similar provision, but they lost them because they put education first.

Did Jesus pick out educated men for His work? He did not. He called fishermen and tax collectors. He passed by the schools and universities. How fearful would have been the loss if Moody, Gipsy Smith and Philpott had been rejected because they did not take the prescribed course!

Should we accept men because they meet our educational standards, or because they have been called of God and are qualified to do His work? Do their natural gifts and talents count for nothing? Does a college degree qualify a man, or the anointing of the Spirit of God?

Now please do not misunderstand me. I am not opposed to the prescribed course of training. I think everyone who can should take it. But I am speaking now of multitudes for whom it is impossible. Are they to be ignored? Must they be set aside? God forgive us. Think of what the Salvation Army did in its early years with men and women who never earned a degree. Think of Malla Moe who only went through the second grade and yet became one of Africa's greatest soul-winners.

Do you wonder why I feel so keenly about it? Let me tell you. I am one of those who could not take the prescribed course. So far as the denominations were concerned, I was out. They would not accept me for the ministry. Yet God had called me. About that I had no doubt. What then was I to do?

You see, I did not get through public school until I was sixteen. I was always sickly and delicate. Hence, I was out of school a great deal. And I was not a good student. There are many who are not good students. They just do not take to books. They should not be forced to take what they are not fitted to take. Some other course of instruction should be devised for them. The things that interest them are the things they should do. Robert G. LeTourneau was a very poor student but he is one of the world's greatest inventors.

I went to high school for a few weeks, but I got nowhere. I could do nothing with higher mathematics and languages. Latin was a nightmare to me. So I left school and went to work. Later, I went through the Toronto Bible College and just loved it.

It may interest those who have seen or read the twenty-two books I have written, the numerous magazine articles, the six hundred hymns, poems and gospel songs, to know something of the difficulties I encountered at the beginning.

My instructor in literature was a professor at Wycliffe College, and literature was my favourite subject. How I loved to study and, later, teach the poems of Tennyson! I was asked to write a composition for examination. Never will I forget the rebuke of my professor. He took the time to write me a letter. The article I had written was impossible, he said. He would give me fifty marks so that I could pass, but my composition was not worth it. I was poor in punctuation and spelling, poor in grammar and sentence construction. I could never hope to be a writer.

Never will I forget how my uncle, who was president of the Massey-Harris Co., Toronto, tried to get me into Knox College. I remember even now his talk with one of the professors over the telephone. But when he informed him that I had neither high school nor college, his answer was an emphatic no. There was no place in the ministry for anyone unless he could go back to school and take the prescribed course before entering seminary. His earnestness and devotion, his gifts and talents, his consecration and call to preach, made absolutely no difference. No matter how sick he had been, no matter how old he was, he must become a schoolboy again and take the entire course. Nothing else mattered. Nothing else counted. Moody was out. Gipsy Smith was out. A thousand and one others were out, and I was out.

Well now, what was I to do? Must I give up? If only highly educated men could enter the ministry, then how could I get in?

One day I heard about McCormick Theological Seminary, Chicago, one of the largest Presbyterian seminaries in the country. I applied. To my amazement, Dr. James McClure, the President, accepted me. He never even asked about my previous education. I told him God had called me to the ministry and he took me in. He knew I could not tackle Greek and Hebrew, but that I could take everything else, and I did. How I thank God for Dr. McClure and McCormick! He gave me a chance, not knowing whether I would pastor a large church or a small, whether I would succeed or fail.

How I enjoyed the classes, especially those of Dr. Hill, Dr. McAfee, and Dr. Robinson! The work was easy, both literature and theology—easy because I loved it.

Oh, I was not a brilliant student. I was far more interested in the practical work I was doing, my work as a student pastor, preaching and winning souls, than I was in my studies. But I got through, and, finally, after three wonderful years, I was handed my certificate, along with the other members of my class, and my picture was included among the graduates of 1915. I had passed in every subject.

Now, don't misjudge McCormick. McCormick has its scholastic standards. Of course it has. Most of my fellow students had a B.A. But Dr. McClure made an exception. He let down the bars. He believed I would make good, and he took me in. God bless him for it!

I was ordained by the Chicago Presbytery. Then I returned to Canada and was transferred to the Toronto Presbytery, and, after a few months of special work in Knox College, I was duly accepted as a minister of the Presbyterian Church of Canada. But if it had not been for McCormick, where would I be? What chance would I have had?

For a quarter of a century now it has been my privilege to preach to one of the largest congregations in all Canada. The Peoples Church is at present providing the personal support for over three hundred and fifty missionaries on the foreign field. My evangelism has taken me to fifty-three countries around the world in city-wide campaigns. God has permitted me to write some twenty-two books which have had a world-wide circulation in more than a score of different languages. I have seen hundreds upon hundreds of young people go into Christian service. All this would have been lost had I been compelled to take the prescribed course.

It is not what a man has in his head that counts; it is what he has in his heart. It is not his learning; it is his spiritual power. I have dealt with thousands of young people and, important as education is, I have always put their ability to do the job first. Some men can make good without the prescribed course of study, while others cannot make good with it.

Moreover, anyone who will apply himself can educate himself by becoming a student at home. He can read Miller's *Church History* until he has mastered it. He can study *The Annotated Bible* by Gaebelein until he really knows the Word of God. He can find out "How We Got Our Bible" and learn a little about "Archaeology", etc., from Halley's *Pocket Bible Handbook*. He can study *The Great Doctrines of the Bible* by Evans. He can gather inspiration from the biographies of the great missionaries, revivalists, evangelists and reformers of the past. He can study evangelism from *The Consuming Fire* by Oswald J. Smith. He can secure a Scofield Reference Bible. He may not agree with all the notes, but he will have a course of study second-to-none. Above all, I would urge him to live with Wesley's Veterans until he knows every preacher who laboured in the greatest spiritual movement since Pentecost. Thus he can become a self-taught man—if he will.

In conclusion, I will always urge young people to take the regular course, if possible, but I will always send those who are too old, or converted too late, or who for some other reason have failed to qualify, to some good Bible school where they can make up for their deficiencies and secure a training that will equip them for God's service. There have always been exceptions to the rule, and there always will be. We must never fail to make provision for these exceptions. They may become our most successful workers.

CHAPTER IX

MAN AND THIS MODERN AGE

YOU will find my text in the Book of Job, the twenty-fifth chapter and the fourth verse: "How then can man be justified with God?"

That question was asked by Bildad in his third discourse. It leads me to ask and answer a number of questions, and as I do so, I think we will get the answer to our text: "How then can man be justified with God?"

1. *Why don't you preach a social gospel?*

My friend, if a social gospel would save, then I would preach it. But man needs life. Social service, education, reformation, a better environment will not give it. You may put a pig in your parlour if you will, but instead of the parlour turning the pig into a respectable animal, the pig will turn the parlour into a pig-sty. You may dress a private in an officer's uniform but he is still a private.

No, my friend, no social gospel can impart life, and man, I say, needs life. You may plough, harrow, cultivate and roll the ground until it is beautiful, but it will be all in vain unless you put in the seed. There must be life— all else is inadequate. Regeneration is absolutely imperative. "Ye must be born again." There is no power in a social gospel to justify man with God.

If all man needed was improvement, a better environment, education, then I might preach a social gospel, but when I know perfectly well that man needs life—eternal life—and that unless he can get that life he will be lost and lost forever, then I am not going to preach a social gospel. I will leave that to the Government, to the politicians, to those who believe in world betterment. I want a message that will impart life. That is why God says "He that hath the Son hath life; and he that hath not the Son of God hath not life" (1 John 5: 12). Only Jesus Christ can impart life.

Therefore, my friend, I do not urge you to clean up, I urge you to accept Christ. I do not tell you to turn over a new leaf, I tell you to receive Jesus. He will take care of the new life once He gets into your heart. He will change you completely. But you must be changed on the inside before you can be changed on the outside. I say, I do not preach a social gospel, because no social gospel can impart life, it cannot meet man's need.

2. Why can't I indulge in worldly pleasures and amusements?

I suppose you are thinking of drinking, smoking, going to shows, card playing, etc. Well, now, my friend, if you are unsaved, there is no reason why you should not indulge in these things, if you want to. If you are willing to pay the price and suffer the consequences, well, it is up to you. You might as well commit one sin as another. Dancing, theatre-going, card-playing belong to the world, and if you are not a Christian then that, of course, is your life and no one is going to blame you for indulging in these things. So, I say, if you are unsaved, you can—why not?

If, on the other hand, you are a Christian, then you will do everything to the glory of God. Now let me ask you a question. Can you drink to God's glory? Can you smoke to God's glory? Can you sit in a theatre, or a moving-picture show and have communion and fellowship with God? Can you play a game of cards and dance and at the same time ask God's blessing upon what you are doing? If you can, then there is no reason why you should not. All you have to do is to ask one question—Can I do this for God's glory? Will God be glorified if I do it? And if He will, then there is no reason why you should not do it.

But if, on the other hand, you cannot do it to the glory of God, if you know perfectly well that when you do these things you are out of fellowship with God, if you realize that you are bringing no honour to His name, then they become a sin, and you should abstain. As a matter of fact, you *will* abstain, if you have been born again. You will experience the expulsive power of a new affection. Christ will mean so much to you that the love for the world will be gone. You will no longer love the world that crucified your Lord. You will take your stand against the world and all it represents, and you will be out and out for God.

I answer your question, therefore, by quoting 1 Corinthians 10: 31: "Whether therefore ye eat, or drink, or whatsoever ye do, do all to the glory of God." If you belong to the world then you have a right to indulge in the things of the world, but if you belong to God then you should take part in the things that glorify Him. You should do nothing that would bring dishonour on His Name. I have never known a man who has indulged in these things who has been a soul winner, a revivalist, or a man of prayer. They just don't go together. You must be either one thing or the other.

3. *Why doesn't my conscience trouble me now like it used to?*

My friend, you may have so many stains on your dress that another makes very little difference. Sin is no longer sinful once you have become used to it. You see, you have silenced conscience by refusing to listen to it so often that you no longer hear it. It is like an alarm clock. First you heard it and you turned it off immediately, but finally you ignored it and now it can ring loud and long and it doesn't even awaken you.

It is possible for the Spirit to be quenched, and when He is quenched He will no longer speak. He has tried to faithfully warn you but you have ignored His warnings. That is why you are not convicted like you used to be. When you first committed that sin you felt dreadful. You will never forget it. But you committed it again, and then again, and finally you committed it so often that now it doesn't bother you and you can commit it without your conscience being aroused. You do not feel the condemnation that you once felt. You do not suffer as you once did. The contrition that you experienced years ago, you no longer experience. You do not cry to God in penitence and sorrow as you once did. Why not? You have silenced conscience, you have quenched the Spirit, you are getting to a place where God can no longer speak to you. You are in a most dangerous position. That, my friend, is why you are not troubled as you once were.

4. *Why can't I act like Christ?*

You cannot act like Christ because you have never been born into the family of God. I act like a Smith, I walk like a Smith, I talk like a Smith. But I act and walk and talk like a Smith because I am a Smith. I was born into the family. I act like my father because I was born of my father. The reason, my friend, that you do not act like Christ is because you have not been born of Christ. If you had been born of Christ then you would act as He does.

You see, whatever you are on the inside you will be on the outside. If Christ indwells, He will manifest Himself and others will see Jesus in you. The orange tree does not struggle to bear oranges. It is never worried for fear it might make a mistake and grow crab-apples. It has the juice of the orange in its bark. It is most natural for it to grow oranges. No effort is necessary. So it is with you. If you are filled with the Holy Spirit; if Christ indwells in all His glorious fulness, then He will manifest Himself without. He will reproduce His own life from within. You do not live the Christian life. No one ever has, no one ever can, no one ever will. The Christian life is the outliving of the indwelling Christ. If Christ indwells, then the Christian life will be lived.

Moreover, it is not lived by you, it is lived by Christ. You are merely the vehicle, the channel. Therefore if you have been truly born again, and Jesus Christ indwells, He will manifest Himself and everyone will know that you are a Christian. Christ reproduces His own life from within. You do not have to try to live the Christian life, you just let go and let Him live it. So you had better ask yourself the question: Does Christ indwell?

5. *Why can't I be saved by doing my best?*

That is a question a great many people are asking. They want to know why they cannot be saved by obeying the Golden Rule; by observing the law of Moses; by living up to the ethics and principles of the Bible. My friend, that is absolutely impossible. No man can justify himself.

We come now to the heart of the question. "How then can man be justified with God?" Suppose we answer Bildad's question.

There are only two religions in this world of ours— man's religion and God's religion. There are no others. Man's religion is by works—by his own efforts, his own endeavours. Man tries to become his own saviour; he wants to save himself. It doesn't matter how that religion is expressed, whether in Roman Catholicism, Mahommedanism, Confucianism, Buddhism, or Protestantism—it is all the same. The man who, by his own works and efforts, long prayers and pilgrimages, his fastings, his good deeds, is trying to save himself, is following his own religion.

On the other hand, there is God's religion, or rather God's salvation. Then Jesus Christ becomes the Saviour. You see, man has a disease—he has a sin cancer. What would be the good of a book on the laws of health in a sanatorium? Suppose he were to live up to all of them, he would still be sick. No law could cure him. The only way he could be cured would be to have someone take his disease and give him his health.

That, my friend, is what Jesus Christ did nineteen hundred years ago. He took your disease, your sin, loathsome as it was. He took it into His own body on the tree and bore it as He hung there on Calvary's Cross. He died in your stead and room. Your sin was laid on Him, "The Lord hath laid on him the iniquity of us all" (Isa. 53: 6).

But not only did He die and bear your sins, He rose from the dead. He rose triumphant over the grave. And now He lives to save. Now he can give you His health, His life. In exchange for your sin He gives you eternal life. That was the way He justified you. He made a complete and perfect atonement for your sin.

6. *What now do I have to do?*

All you have to do now is to open your heart and accept Him as your own personal Saviour, and when you do you will be born again. And when you are born again, you will turn away from sin. Sin will have no attraction for you. The things you once loved, you will hate ; the things you once hated, you will now love. You will be saved, not by keeping the law, the Mosaic law or any other law, not by doing your best—you will be saved by Jesus Christ. You will be saved by a Person, the Son of the living God, the resurrected living Saviour.

"How then can man be justified with God?" By turning from all reliance upon himself and his own efforts to save him, and by trusting Jesus Christ, the Lamb of God who bore away the sin of the world. By opening his heart to Jesus Christ and receiving Him as his own personal Saviour. By turning from all reliance upon religion or good works, and by relying wholly upon Christ. There is no other way.

My friend, have I answered your questions? You know now why I do not preach a social gospel. You know now why you cannot indulge in worldly pleasures and amusements. You know now why your conscience doesn't trouble you like it used to. You know now why you cannot act like Christ. And you know now why you cannot be saved by doing your best. You know that your only hope is in Jesus Christ, the risen, resurrected Saviour.

Well now, what are you going to do about it? Are you ready to receive Jesus Christ as your Saviour? Are you prepared to turn from all your reliance upon everything else and trust Him and Him alone? Will you at this moment open your heart and accept Him? There is no time like the present. God holds out no hope of the future. It may be now or never, so far as you are concerned. Oh, then, receive Him. Will you do it? Do it, and do it *NOW*.

CHAPTER X

GOD AND THIS MODERN AGE

MY text is found in Daniel, the second chapter, and the twenty-eighth verse: "There is a God in heaven." That statement is absolutely true. I know the fool says there is no God, but the Bible says: "There is a God in heaven."

Now let me answer a number of questions in order to bring you into touch with God. Let me show you why you have not yet found Him, and why you do not know Him, and then let me show you how you can know Him.

1. *Why has science never discovered God?*

The reason science has never discovered God, my friend, is because God cannot be discovered; God is revealed: "The world by wisdom knew not God" (1 Cor. 1: 21). Science works in the realm of the intellect and reason. God is known in experience. The Bible says: "Taste and see." If you do, you will know that "there is a God in heaven".

Now if you try to discover God in the realm of science, reason, wisdom, you will never discover Him. He is not there. God does not promise a discovery by any such means. If, on the other hand, you are ready to know God in experience, you will know Him. You must "taste and see" for yourself. The trouble is, you have never tasted, you have never seen, you have never experienced God.

Man has been trying for centuries to find God. There are men today who are searching for God. Why, then, do they not find Him? Many of them are honest in their search. The trouble is, God cannot be found. God cannot be discovered. God must be revealed. And not until God reveals Himself to you, will you ever know Him. Well, now, how can God be revealed? What can you do about it? Let us see if we cannot find out. If "there is a God in heaven" there must be a way to contact Him.

2. *How do you know that there is a God when you have never seen Him?*

One time a famous doctor said he had never seen a soul though he had dissected hundreds of bodies, and, therefore, he concluded, there is no such thing as a soul. What foolishness! My friend, you can't see love, but you know that love exists. You can't see hate, but you know that there is such a thing as hate. There are a lot of things you cannot see that you know are real. You know that there is such a country as China, but you have never seen China. You know that there is such a place as the North Pole, but you have never seen the North Pole. How do you know, then, that they exist? I suppose, just because others have told you about them. Well, have not others told you about God? Is there not an entire Book written about Him? Why do you believe one and not the other? What a foolish argument. Of course "there is a God in heaven".

3. *Why have men failed to find God?*

One reason they have failed to find God is because they haven't travelled far enough. There are some things that you have to travel a long way to find. Man hasn't travelled very far. The Bible says God is in heaven.

May I ask you to turn to Psalm 139? Suppose we read verses 7–10, and see whether or not we have gone far enough: "Whither shall I go from thy spirit? or whither shall I flee from thy presence? If I ascend up into heaven, thou art there: if I make my bed in hell, behold, thou art there. If I take the wings of the morning, and dwell in the uttermost parts of the sea; Even there shall thy hand lead me, and thy right hand shall hold me."

Now, my friend, let me ask you a few questions, based on the passage we have just read. Have you ascended into heaven? Well, that's where God is, and if you want to find God, you will have to travel a little farther. "There

is a God in heaven." Have you ever gone to hell? The
psalmist says that God can be found in hell, or, as it is
in the original—sheol. If you were to go to sheol you
would be convinced of the fact that there is a God. Have
you gone to the uttermost parts of the sea? All you have
to do is to go far enough and you will find God. You are
limited in your knowledge because you have travelled in
a very narrow circle.

4. *Why don't I enjoy the things of God?*

Why don't you enjoy your food? There are only two
reasons. You do not enjoy your food simply because you
are either sick or dead. A dead man cannot enjoy food
and, as a rule, a sick man does not enjoy food. Now, if
you do not know God, if you have never been saved, if
you have never been born again, if you have never passed
out of death and into life, if you do not have eternal life,
then, my friend, you are dead and you never will enjoy
the things of God. You are still in the world and you will
enjoy the things of this life, the things of this world. You
enjoy the environment in which you live. If you live in
the world, then that is the environment you will enjoy.
If you were alive, you would enjoy the things of God.
It may be, therefore, that you have never been saved,
that you do not know God, that you are dead, and, therefore, you do not enjoy God.

However, you may know God, but you may be sick.
You may be a back-slider, you may have wandered afar
off, you may not be reading the Bible or praying. You
may be indulging in sin. You may not be living the life
that God wants you to live. You may, I say, be sick, and
just as a sick person does not enjoy food, so a sick
Christian does not enjoy the things of God. My friend, you
had better come back, you had better get right, for unless
you do, you will never again enjoy the things of the Lord.

There was a time when you enjoyed the prayer meeting
and loved to testify. You enjoyed singing the gospel
hymns; you were most active in personal work; you
loved to attend evangelistic meetings; you enjoyed sing-

ing in the choir. Now you no longer enjoy these things. Why not? You have lost your testimony, you have backslidden. You are not where you once were. You are not interested in the things of God, because you are now a sick Christian.

5. *How can a loving God send men to hell?*

God does not send men to hell. My friend, you are on an incline and you are sliding into hell. Nineteen hundred years ago God threw His only begotten Son across the incline to save you. If you go to hell now, you will have to go over Him. "There is a God in heaven", and He has done everything He can to prevent you from sliding into hell.

Hell was made for the devil and his angels, not for man. God never intended that man should go to hell. But if man follows the devil in this life, then he will have to follow him in eternity. God has no place but heaven for His own. If you belong to Satan, then you will some day find yourself in hell. God in His love and mercy has done everything possible to keep you from going to hell.

Nineteen hundred years ago He gave His only begotten Son to die on Calvary's Cross that you might not perish. So great was His love that He allowed His Son to suffer and to die that an atonement might be made. You did not even ask Him to do it. He did it before you were even born. He did it of His own free will. He did it because He is "not willing that any should perish" but that all might come and have life. He does not want you to be lost. Jesus came to seek and to save the lost.

Just as the woman went in search of the coin; just as the father welcomed home his prodigal son; just as Jesus sought the woman at the well, so God seeks you. You are not seeking Him, He is seeking you. He always has been seeking you.

6. *What must I do that I may know God?*

Do you not realize that your back has been turned toward God, and that God's face has been turned toward you? God calls upon you to right-about-face. Instead of going away from Him, go *to* Him. "For God so loved the world that he gave his only begotten Son, that whosoever believeth in him, should not perish but have everlasting life" (John 3: 16). That is the Gospel, my friend. God gave His Son, so great was His love. He does not want you to perish. If you will believe in Him, if you will trust Him, you will not perish. Instead, you will know that "there is a God in heaven" and you will have everlasting life.

Tell me, do you want to perish? Do you want to be lost? Or do you want life eternal, the life of the ages? Do you not want to live forever? Do you not want to spend eternity with the Lord Jesus? Then come, acknowledge that you are a sinner, acknowledge that you are lost, acknowledge that you need a Saviour, open your heart to Jesus Christ and receive Him. Then thank Him for your salvation, for what He did for you on Calvary's Cross, and for what He does for you now in saving your soul. Why should you perish? Why should you go to hell? Provision has been made. God will have mercy and abundantly pardon. Will you then receive Christ? Do it, and do it NOW.

CHAPTER XI

HOW CAN AN HONEST SCEPTIC BE CONVINCED OF A FUTURE LIFE?

TURN, if you will, to Isaiah 1: 15: "Come now, and let us reason together, saith the Lord."

My friend, we are going to reason together. As a matter of fact, God has challenged you to reason with Him. How can an honest sceptic be convinced of a future life? Let me tell you. Let me reason with you.

1. *The possibility that there is a future life should lead us to make a most careful investigation*

We must start there. You must admit, to begin with, that there may possibly be a future life. In other words, there could be a future life. If so, then you should be willing to make a most careful investigation. Are you willing? Do you admit the possibility of a future life? If so, then let God reason with you, and before long you will be sure.

2. *No one has ever proved that there is not a future life*

Man has been on this earth now for at least six thousand years, and up to this present hour not a single individual has been able to prove that there is *not* a future life. Scientists, atheists, philosophers have endeavoured to prove it and have failed. No one has brought forth any positive proof. Therefore, I say, the fact that there is not a future life has never been proved. That you will have to admit.

3. *God invites us to reason about it*

Now I come to my text: "Come now, and let us reason together, saith the Lord." Are you willing to let God reason with you? If you are, you will soon be convinced.

Of that I am certain. If then you are willing to let God reason with you, we will go on from this point, step by step, until at last you will not only admit the possibility of a future life, but you will be convinced that there is a future life.

4. *Most sceptics reason against a future life, in order to get away from God; very few reason for it, in order to get to God*

Am I not right? Is it not true that most of the sceptics that you have known have set out to reason against a future life and have done so in order to get away from God? How many, I wonder, have been anxious to really get to God? How many have reasoned in order to find out the facts, and how many have welcomed the facts when they have found them?

What about yourself? Why have you read so many books by sceptics and atheists? There is just one answer —you want arguments against God, against a future life. If you wanted arguments for God and for a future life, you would read the Bible. You would not read the books of the sceptics. If you are honest, you will reason with a sincere desire to be convinced of a future life and to get in touch with God.

Now God has His own plans for finding out about a future life. The trouble is, most of us want to follow our own plans. We have our own way of reasoning. That is why we have never yet succeeded—we will not reason God's way. God has a way of His own. He wants you to reason His way. If you are honest, you will. Now suppose you stop right now and ask yourself whether or not you are honest. Are you willing to reason God's way?

5. *God has promised to reveal Himself to those who are honest and sincere*

"And ye shall seek me, and find me, when ye shall search for me with all your heart" (Jer. 29: 13). My friend, God tells you very plainly in this verse, taken from the Bible, His Book, that you can find Him if you will seek Him, if you will search for Him with all your heart. Now tell me, have you ever done it? Or has all your searching been to get away from God? Have you ever searched in order to get to God, and have you searched with all your heart? Will you now put your whole heart into it, in order that you may not be disappointed? God says you can find Him if you will. Stop right now and ask yourself whether or not you are really sincere, and whether or not you are searching for Him with all your heart.

You see, if you are against the truth to begin with, then you are not honest, and you cannot hope to get to God. You cannot expect to know about a future life. If you start out by trying to find arguments to disprove a future life, to disprove the existence of God, you are not honest. You must seek Him with all your heart and be really anxious to find Him.

Do you remember the Queen of Sheba, in the days of Solomon? She travelled many miles to make a careful, honest investigation. Notice the statement, if you will, in Matthew 12: 42: "The queen of the south shall rise up in judgment with this generation, and shall condemn it: for she came from the uttermost parts of the earth to hear the wisdom of Solomon: and, behold, a greater than Solomon is here." Now, my friend, the day may come— as a matter of fact, the day *will* come—when God will condemn you. You should at least do what the Queen of Sheba did. You should be anxious enough and sincere enough to find out. She came from the uttermost parts of the earth to hear the wisdom of Solomon. She was not disappointed. Jesus, this verse says, is greater than Solomon. If the Queen of Sheba would go so far to find out about Solomon, surely you should go as far to find out about the Lord Jesus Christ.

6. *What now is God's method?*

You will find God's method stated in John 7: 17: "If any man will do his will, he shall know of the doctrine, whether it be of God, or whether I speak of myself." The question is, are you willing to do God's will? If you are not willing to do His will, then you may as well stop in your search right where you are, but if you are honest, then you will be willing to do His will, when you know it. And God says that if you are willing then you will know about the doctrine—the doctrine of a future life, or any other doctrine—you will know whether it is merely human or whether it is of God. You will know whether Jesus speaks as a man, or whether He speaks as God. I say, you will know, you will be convinced, that is, if you are honest, if you are willing to do His will.

That is the one and only condition. I am afraid the average sceptic is not willing to do God's will. He doesn't want to turn from his sin, he doesn't want to live for God, he doesn't want to believe, he doesn't want to be convinced. No sceptic who has been willing to do God's will has ever been disappointed. God will reveal Himself to you, my friend, if you are willing to do His will. But, are you willing? That is for you to say. You can get nowhere unless you come God's way. But if you will, you will not be disappointed.

Now what is God's will? In other words, what is His commandment? About this we are left in no doubt. It is clearly stated in I John 3: 23. Let me read it to you: "And this is his commandment, That we should *believe* on the name of his Son Jesus Christ." That is the will of God. He commands you to believe on the name of His Son Jesus Christ. Are you willing then to believe? Oh, I know what you are saying. You are saying you can't believe. That, my friend, is not true. The difficulty is not with your head, it is with your heart, your will. The question is, Are you willing to believe?

If God reveals Jesus Christ to you, will you believe in Him? Will you come in that attitude? If you set yourself against Him, then He can do nothing for you. If you are unwilling to believe, He cannot help you. You must be prepared to do His will. You must be *willing* to believe. Now, tell me, are you willing? Can you honestly say that you want to do the will of God? If you do, then the battle has been won. He commands you to believe on His Son.

He will enable you to believe if you are willing. Can you say with the centurion of old: "Lord, I believe; help thou mine unbelief"?

Note also Hosea 6: 3: "Then shall we know, if we follow on to know the Lord." Don't give up, follow on, persevere. The results are absolutely certain. God says that if you follow on, you will know Him. You will know Him personally, you will be convinced; but you will have to follow on.

Now what was John's method? Here it is: "But these are written, that ye might believe that Jesus is the Christ, the Son of God; and that believing ye might have life through his name" (John 20: 31).

My friend, all you have to do is to read what has been written. In other words, read John's Gospel. I have never known anyone, whether sceptic or not, who has sincerely, earnestly, honestly, read the Gospel of John, slowly, from beginning to end, who has not been convinced. John's Gospel is the Gospel of the Son of God. It is the Gospel of faith. It is the Gospel that proves beyond the slightest shadow of a doubt that there is a future life, that Jesus Christ came from God, that He went back to God, that He gave His life on Calvary's Cross to become man's Saviour, and that tells you how to be saved.

It makes it clear that God does not want you to perish, that He offers you eternal life through His Son, and that all you have to do is to trust Jesus Christ; in other words, receive Him as your own personal Saviour. John says that his whole purpose in writing this Gospel was in order that men might believe that Jesus was indeed the Christ, the Son of God, and that believing, they might have life through His Name. And that is exactly what happens. When you believe in Jesus Christ; when you receive Him as your Saviour, you have life, eternal life.

Now, my friend, let me urge you to read the Gospel of John. There is no book like it in the entire universe. It is the greatest Book that has ever been written. Sit down quietly, hour by hour, day by day, and read through John's Gospel from beginning to end, and read it through three or four times, and I guarantee that if you are an honest sceptic, you will be convinced beyond the slightest shadow of a doubt—you will know that there is a future life, you will know that there is a God, you will know that Jesus Christ is His Son. And if you will accept Christ as your Saviour, you will have eternal life. You will be saved, saved for time and eternity.

7. *Are you willing now to come God's way?*

Do you know that of thirty of the greatest sceptics who wrote against God and the Bible when they were young, no less than twenty-eight of them accepted Christ when they were older? I repeat, out of thirty of the greatest sceptics who wrote against God and the Bible when they were young, no less than twenty-eight of them accepted Christ as their Saviour when they were older. How do you account for it? How do you explain it?

Perhaps you are not as young as you used to be. The years have come and gone, and today you are older. When you were young, you laughed at God. You ridiculed the idea of a future life. Now that you are older you realize that you are drawing nearer to the end. Some day it will all be over. Perhaps you wonder whether you will die as an animal, or whether you will have to face God. Perhaps you wonder whether this life ends all, or whether there is, after all, a future life. You are worried, you are concerned, you want to know.

My friend, if twenty-eight of the greatest sceptics were convinced of a future life when they were older, and if they accepted Jesus Christ as their Saviour, and if only two did not, then, if I were you, I would follow the example of the twenty-eight, rather than the example of the two. I would accept Christ and be saved.

Will you now come God's way? Have you allowed God to reason with you? What more can I say? I have given you John 7: 17. I have told you that that is God's method. I have asked you to be willing to do God's will, because God has promised if you are, you will know. I have given you Hosea 6: 3. I have urged you to persevere. Last of all, I have given you John 20: 31. I have suggested that you read John's Gospel from beginning to end. I have told you that if you will, you will be convinced. Well now, will you do it?

The trouble is not with your head but with your will. Jesus said: "Ye will not come to me" (John 5: 40). It isn't that you cannot, you *will* not. You can if you will. You tell me you cannot believe? That is not true. God says you will not.

Oh, my friend, let me beg of you to open your heart to the Lord Jesus Christ—the One who gave His life on Calvary's Cross for you, and receive Him as your own personal Saviour. He will set you free from every sin. He will take away the cobwebs that clog your mind. He will enable you to believe. If you will come God's way, you will be saved. You will know that there is a future life. And if Jesus Christ becomes your Saviour, you will spend eternity in Heaven, where you will enjoy that future life and enjoy it for evermore. Will you do it? Do it, and do it NOW.

CHAPTER XII

FIVE TREMENDOUS TRUTHS

YOU will find my text in Jonah, the second chapter, and the ninth verse: "Salvation is of the Lord." I am not going to deal with the story of Jonah. Rather I am going to present five tremendous truths which prove conclusively that Salvation, as Jonah declared, is of the Lord.

1. *All men are lost and on their way to perdition, because all men are sinners in the sight of God*

That is the first tremendous truth, and what a truth it is. It is true indeed that all men are lost and on their way to perdition. The human race is rushing down a precipice toward destruction. God says: "All we like sheep have gone astray; we have turned every one to his own way" (Isa. 53: 6). It is because men are lost that Jesus Christ came to save them. The Bible says: "The Son of man is come to seek and to save that which was lost" (Luke 19: 10).

Now the reason men are lost is because they have sinned against God. I have sinned, you have sinned, all mankind has sinned. There is no one who has lived a sinless life. The Bible says: "All have sinned, and come short of the glory of God" (Rom. 3: 23). "There is none righteous, no, not one" (Rom. 3: 10). Hence, all are sinners in the sight of God.

In speaking of sinners the Bible says: "The wicked is reserved to the day of destruction" (Job 21: 30). "Thou hast destroyed the wicked, thou hast put out their name for ever and ever" (Ps. 9: 5). "The wicked shall be turned into hell, and all the nations that forget God" (Ps. 9: 17). In Psalm 37 we read these statements: "Evildoers shall be cut off: the wicked shall perish: the

74

transgressors shall be destroyed." In Malachi 4: 1 we read: "All that do wickedly, shall be stubble: and the day that cometh shall burn them up, saith the Lord of hosts, that it shall leave them neither root nor branch." Paul says they "shall be punished with everlasting destruction" (2 Thess. 1: 9). Finally, in Revelation 20: 15, we read: "And whosoever was not found written in the book of life was cast into the lake of fire."

So then there is no hope for those out of Christ. The wicked are to perish. All whose names are not in the book of life will be lost, and lost forever. They have sinned against God, they have rejected Jesus Christ and now they are doomed.

My friend, will you be there? Are you to be numbered with the wicked? Then for you there is no hope. You are lost, and on your way to perdition. You may not believe it now but you will experience it hereafter. Therefore, trifle not. Your doom is sure. If you go on as you are, there is no hope. You are condemned for all eternity. Right now you are a lost soul, headed for destruction, for you have sinned against Almighty God. The lake of fire will be your doom, the second death your eternal destiny. You will be consigned to hell, along with all the nations that forget God.

You tell me you are not a great sinner. What difference does it make? If you have sinned, you have sinned. No sin can enter Heaven. One transgression will bar you. The fact of the matter is, you are without excuse. You have transgressed the laws of God. You have broken His commandments. You have sinned against your own conscience. You know perfectly well that you are unfit to face a holy God. If you have not yet accepted the Lord Jesus Christ as your own personal Saviour, then you are guilty of the greatest sin a man can commit, for you have spurned the love and mercy of God; you have refused His pardon; you have ignored His Son; you have turned your back on Jesus Christ. Therefore, my friend, there is no hope. You are lost and on your way to perdition because you are a sinner in the sight of God.

You are not a sinner because you sin; you sin because you are a sinner. Your very nature is sinful. You were born in sin, you were shapen in iniquity. An apple tree is not an apple tree because it bears apples; it bears apples because it is an apple tree. You sin because you are already a sinner. You started going astray as soon as you came to the years of responsibilty, and you have been going astray ever since. Hence you must face the wrath of Almighty God, and there is no hope of escape so long as you continue in your present state.

2. *All men are doomed to death, but death is followed by judgment, from which there is no escape.*

The Bible says: "The wages of sin is death" (Rom. 6: 23). "The soul that sinneth, it shall die" (Ez. 18: 4). Death is therefore the outcome of sin. Death is the penalty. When I speak of death I am not referring to the death of the body, but to the death of the soul. I am not referring to the first death, but to the second death. If you, my friend, have only been born once, then you will have to die twice. It is only those who have been born twice who will die but once. What could be worse than eternal death? Are you willing to face it? Have you no fear in your heart? Do you not dread the thought of it? Would you not flee from it if you could? Think of it—death, your eternal doom.

The Bible says: "It is appointed unto men once to die, but after this the judgment" (Heb. 9: 27). Now the awful thing about physical death is the fact that it is followed by judgment, and from judgment there is no escape. A day is coming when every man out of Christ will have to meet God. Judgment is certain. Sooner or later there must be a judgment, a judgment over which Jesus Christ Himself will be the presiding judge. Today He is presented as a Saviour, but, if men will not have Him as a Saviour, then they will be compelled to face Him as a judge. God has committed all judgment to His Son (John 5: 21). Jesus, who Himself became man, will be the judge of man.

It is bad enough to be arraigned in an earthly court before an earthly judge, but what will it be to stand before the judge of all mankind and to know that the sentence He pronounces will be final? There can be no appeal to a higher court. His court is the highest of all. Moreover, His judgment will be absolutely righteous, because He knows the hearts of men. He will be impartial. No one will be able to hide anything from Him. He knows all that we have done, all that we have said, and all that we have thought. He knows our very motives.

All who do not know Christ will be arraigned before Him. "It is a fearful thing to fall into the hands of the living God" (Heb. 10: 31). The very thought of it ought to make us tremble. Our hearts should be filled with dread and alarm. Think of having all your thoughts exposed, not only before your friends, but before the entire universe. Think of having no answer, no excuse. Are you prepared to face it? Will you go into the presence of God unsaved? Would you have Him as your judge? All men, I say, are doomed to death, but death is followed by judgment, from which there is no escape.

3. *No man can be saved by his works of righteousness, nor can the Church deliver him from his doom*

All men are lost. All men are on their way to hell. All men have sinned against God. All men are doomed to death. All men must face the judgment, a judgment from which there can be no escape. Now let us go on— what next? No man can be saved by his works of righteousness, nor can the Church deliver him from his doom.

I am taking it for granted that you do not want to be lost, that you do not want to go to hell, but that you are unprepared to face the judgment, and that you would like to find a way of escape. You are looking now for salvation. You want to know whether or not you can be delivered. Is there any hope? Can you be saved, and if so, how?

First of all, let me make it very clear, my friend, that you cannot be saved by your own works of righteousness. I am not saying that you cannot be saved; I am simply pointing out that your own righteousness cannot save you. Paul, you will remember, turned away from all reliance upon the good life he had lived, realizing that it could not save him. His word was "Not by works of righteousness which we have done" (Titus 3: 5). "Not of works, lest any man should boast" (Eph. 2: 9). No, you cannot do anything to save yourself. It is like trying to lift yourself by your own boot straps. Man can never be his own saviour.

Live the most righteous life that you can live, perform as many good deeds as you can perform, obey the Golden Rule, if you will, observe the ten commandments most meticulously, do the very best you can—all will avail you nothing. Life is not imparted by good works. No deeds of merit, no pilgrimages, no prayers, no works of mercy, nothing that you can do will avail in the least. You cannot buy salvation. You cannot earn salvation. You cannot work for salvation. You cannot achieve salvation. Your own works can never save you.

Even the Church cannot deliver you from your doom. No church ever has, no church ever will. Religion cannot save you. I care not whether it be the Roman Catholic religion, the Protestant religion, the Mohammedan religion, or any other religion—there is no religion that can save. There is no church that can save. Therefore, it makes no difference what church you are a member of, so far as salvation is concerned, because your church cannot save you. You may be a Jew, but Judaism cannot save you. You may be a Roman Catholic, but Roman Catholicism cannot save you. You may be a Protestant, but Protestantism cannot save you. There are no religions that can save. Man is not saved by religion, any more than he is saved by his own righteous acts. Paul was a religious man, but he was not saved by his religious life. Nicodemus was perhaps the most religious Jew that ever lived, but he was not saved by Judaism. Cornelius kept the law blamelessly, but the law could not save him.

You see, my friend, you have a disease. You have a

sin cancer. Something has to be done about that cancer. It would not be sufficient to hand you a book of laws, rules and regulations, and ask you to read them. That would not cure you. It would make no difference what kind of a life you lived, the cancer would still be there. You might become the most religious man on the face of the earth, but the sin cancer would remain. Something, you see, has to be done about the cancer. You can do nothing about it yourself. Your righteousness, your religion, will have no effect on it whatever. Since you are a sinner in the sight of God, a cure must be found. You cannot be your own doctor, your own physician.

That is why I do not urge people to join the Church. I do not want to give them a false sense of security. Too many already are trusting in the Church for salvation. I know perfectly well that the Church cannot save them, and therefore I do not invite them to come forward in order to become members of it. I would be deceiving them if I were to do that. I would be giving them the idea of being saved by uniting with the Church. That, my friend, is absolutely impossible. Church membership has nothing whatever to do with it. You may join all the churches in the world and still be lost, and lost eternally. That is why I say, No man can be saved by his works of righteousness, nor can the Church deliver him from his doom.

4. *Salvation is the gift of God, and it is only by Christ, through faith, that men can be born again*

Now we go a step further. We have seen that men are lost and on their way to perdition because they are sinners in the sight of God. We have seen that they are doomed to death—a death which is followed by judgment, and a judgment from which there can be no escape. We have seen that they cannot be saved by their works of righteousness, and that the Church is unable to deliver them from their doom. Now we come to the next point—Salvation is the gift of God, and it is only by Christ, through faith, that men can be born again.

You see, my friend, you must receive life in order to be saved. You are "dead in trespasses and sins" (Eph. 2: 1). That is why Jesus said to Nicodemus: "Ye must be born again" (John 3: 7). You must receive a new life; a life from above; a life that you have never had before. Your parents gave you natural birth. God, through Christ, offers you spiritual birth.

God's salvation is a gift. If it is a gift it cannot be earned. There is no way to merit it. You cannot work for it. A gift has to be accepted as a gift. You must take God's salvation as you would take a Christmas present. All you can do is to receive it and thank Him for it. The price has already been paid, and it was enormous. God gave His only begotten Son. Jesus shed His life's blood on Calvary's Cross. Jesus bore the penalty for sin. That penalty was death. Jesus gave His life. He made a full and complete atonement, an atonement that satisfied divine justice and met the needs of man.

Suppose I owed a grocery bill which I could not pay. Either someone else would have to pay it for me, or I would have to take the consequences. That is man's situation before God. He owed a debt he could not pay. Jesus Christ stepped in and paid the debt. If man will accept the provision that Christ has made, he may go free.

I point out now that salvation is God's gift. "The gift of God is eternal life through Jesus Christ our Lord" (Rom. 6: 23). "God hath given to us eternal life, and this life is in his Son. He that hath the Son hath life; and he that hath not the Son of God hath not life" (1 John 5: 11, 12). Therefore, if you will accept God's salvation as a gift by accepting Jesus Christ, you will be saved. You see, there is hope for you. You do not have to perish. You may be doomed, but you can escape; that is, if you will accept the mercy of God as it is offered in His Son, Jesus Christ.

Now let me make it perfectly clear that the only way you can accept Christ is by faith. Again and again God offers you salvation by faith in Christ. It is not a head belief, it is a heart belief. It is best expressed by the word

trust. All the intellectual faith in the world will never save
you. You must trust Christ as you trust an elevator, as
you would trust a train, as you would trust a bank. It
must be a practical faith. You must rely wholly upon Him
for time and eternity. In other words, you must receive
Him. The Bible says: "As many as received him, to them
gave he power to become the sons of God" (John 1: 12).
To receive means to do something.

In Revelation 3: 20 it says: "Behold, I stand at the
door, and knock: if any man hear my voice, and open
the door, I will come in" (Rev. 3: 20). You see, Christ
stands on the outside of the door of your heart. The knob
is on the inside. He will not force His way in. You will
have to open the door and let Him in. But the moment
you do, He will come in and you will be saved. Christ
must somehow get into your heart, into your life. When
that happens you are born again, born of the Spirit, born
from above. You have passed from death unto life.
You have received Jesus Christ as your own personal
Saviour, and, trusting Him, you are saved for time and
eternity.

Hence, you do not have to be lost. You need not
perish. You will never have to stand before the great
white throne of judgment, not if you know Christ. Has
that experience, my friend, been your experience? Have
you been converted? When did it happen, where did it
happen, how did it happen? What took place when it
happened? Was there a change, were you transformed?
Does the Spirit at this moment bear witness with your
spirit that you are God's child? Are you standing by faith
on the Word of God? If not, then I beg of you to receive
Him right now. Take Christ as your Saviour. Trust Him,
and trust Him in your heart.

Your intellect, you see, has nothing whatever to do
with it. It doesn't matter what you think or what you
believe; all that matters is: Have you received the Lord
Jesus Christ as your Saviour, have you trusted Him, have
you put your faith in the Son of God, and are you now
His child? That is why I say, Salvation is the gift of God

F

and it is only by Christ, through faith, that men can be born again.

Thus Jesus Christ becomes your Saviour. You are saved, you see, by a Person. It is like a drowning man— he has to have a rescuer. Someone must dive in and save him. What has that to do with your own righteous living? What has that to do with your church membership? You have to be saved by a person and that Person the Lord Jesus Christ. If Christ has not saved you, then you are not saved at all, for no one else can. He is the one and only Saviour. That is why God says "He that hath the Son hath life; and he that hath not the Son of God hath not life" (1 John 5: 12). Eternal life is in Christ. He then must become your Saviour.

That is why I chose as my text "Salvation is of the Lord". I have tried to show you that you can be saved. I have also tried to make it clear that you can only be saved by the Lord. You did not provide salvation, He did. If salvation is of the Lord, then what can you do? All that you can do is to accept it. It is provided by God through the Lord Jesus Christ. It is offered to you by God. It is God's salvation. The salvation that you now receive is not your own, it is His. If, therefore, you are saved you will cry out, with Jonah of old, "Salvation is of the Lord".

5. *When men are converted their lives are utterly changed; old things have passed away and all things become new*

Now, where do works come in? They come in to prove that you are saved, to prove to those around you that you have been converted. You work now, not in order to be saved, but because you *are* saved. Your whole life has been changed, and that transformation is seen by everyone. God puts it this way: "If any man be in Christ, he is a new creature: old things are passed away; behold, all things are become new" (2 Cor. 5: 17).

If that has not taken place, then, my friend, there is no evidence that you have ever passed out of death and into life. If you still live the same old life, commit the same sins, and do the things that you have always done; if there has never been a change, then you have never been converted. Worldliness must give way to Godliness, sin to righteousness. "Shew me thy faith without thy works, and I will shew thee my faith by my works" (Jas. 2: 18). Ah, yes, my friend, if you have been saved, there will be works.

The man who has been addicted to drink, will drink no more, he will become a teetotaller. The man who has used tobacco, will lay it aside. God will deliver him from it. The man who has attended the movies and the theatre, will turn away; he will have no desire for them. The man who has been accustomed to swear and curse, will be given a clean tongue. The man who has indulged in impurity, will now be pure. If you were a saloon keeper when you were saved, you will get into another business. If you were an actor or an actress when you were saved, you will find something else to do—you will get out of the show business. If you hobnobbed with the world, you will now live a separated life. God's Word is clear: "Be ye not unequally yoked together with unbelievers . . . Come out from among them, and be ye separate" (2 Cor. 6: 14, 17). I do not believe in a salvation that does not change a man's life and make him a new creature. If he is new within, he will be new without.

Christ will now become the centre of his life. He will live in the Lord. God will be in his thoughts day and night. He will turn to the Word of God and find the greatest of satisfaction in poring over the pages of the Bible. He will give himself to prayer, and he will find communion with God his chief delight. When he gets the opportunity, he will testify before others and let them know that Christ is in his heart, that he has been delivered from his sin. He will do what he can to serve God. If God calls him to preach, he will preach. If he hears the call to the mission field, he will go. Wherever God wants him, he will serve. He will do the things that God wants him to do.

Henceforth his will will not be at cross purposes with God's will. His will will be parallel with the will of God. He will say with the Lord Jesus Christ, "My meat is to do the will of him that sent me" (John 4: 34). It will be the expulsive power of a new affection. When Christ comes in, the world goes out. When the Holy Spirit takes possession, sin loses its power and old habits drop off. There will be a cleavage. He will draw a line of demarkation. He will put the world on one side and God on the other side, and he will not cross that line. His life will be an example to others—he will no longer be a stumbling block.

Christians who indulge in worldly amusements are not used of God. They never become revivalists. God does not honour them in His service. They have no power in prayer. They do not win souls. Their example does not attract others to Christ. They are powerless and useless in the work of God. Their lives do not count. God wants warriors. There is a battle to be fought. It is the battle between darkness and light, sin and righteousness. It is a battle known only to those who have been born again and are indwelt by the Spirit of God. Only those who have turned from every sin and have renounced the old life entirely, have the courage to engage in this warfare.

My friend, what kind of a Christian are you? Have you been saved, and does your life prove it? Are you living wholly for God? Are you out and out for the Lord Jesus Christ? Have old things passed away and all things become new? If not, I think I would doubt my salvation. I would wonder whether or not I had really been born again, whether or not I had been converted. I urge you to lay your all on the altar, to surrender everything to the Lord Jesus, and to be what He wants you to be. There is no other life worth while, no other life worth living.

Some day it will be all over and you will go to be with Him. You will see Him face to face. You will receive the reward that He has for you. He will welcome you to Heaven, that is if you have been faithful, if you have been true, if you have gone without the camp with Him, bearing His reproach. That is the kind of a Christian God wants you to be. Are you that kind?

"Salvation is of the Lord." I have told you that men are lost and on their way to perdition because they are sinners. I have pointed out that they are doomed to death, a death which will be followed by judgment, and a judgment from which there is no escape. I have told you that your own righteousness can never save you and that the Church is unable to deliver you. I have pointed out that salvation is God's gift through Christ, and that you receive Christ by faith; that only then are you born again. I have urged you to accept Christ as your Saviour. Last of all, I have made it clear that when you are saved, your life will be utterly changed and you will be a new creature in Christ Jesus.

Have I made it plain? Have I made it clear? Then what about you? Where are you? Are you saved or are you lost? If you are lost, then will you not, right now, receive Jesus Christ as your own personal Saviour, that He may deliver you from all sin and save you eternally? I urge you to do it. If "Salvation is of the Lord", then you must know the Lord. To know Him you must accept Him. Will you do it? Do it, and do it—NOW.

CHAPTER XIII

WHO ARE JEHOVAH'S WITNESSES AND WHAT DO THEY TEACH?

THIS false cult was founded by the self-styled "Pastor" Russell, in 1844. After his death in 1916 it was carried on by "Judge" Rutherford (never a judge in any court). He died in 1942, leaving the leadership to one, Nathan H. Knorr.

It has been known by a dozen different names; among them "Russellism", "Millennial Dawnism", "Zion's Watch Tower", "International Bible Students", and now "Jehovah's Witnesses".

It has been propagated by millions of copies of books in some thirty different languages; books in which there is no mention of such spiritual leaders as Luther, Wesley, Finney, Spurgeon, or Moody, for all clergy are alike condemned.

The writers quote an abundance of Scripture, but only their own pet passages, and these are repeated again and again. Most of them are from the Old Testament; very few from the New. They ignore, misappropriate, or interpret symbolically, all Scripture that contradicts their erroneous teachings. Then they proclaim certain truths which all evangelicals hold, with the arrogant insinuation that they are the only ones teaching them.

Now let us examine their false doctrines and answer their erroneous teachings:

1. *Like Spiritism, Christian Science, Christadelphianism and most other false cults, they deny the deity of Jesus*

They claim that before His birth He was an archangel created by God; that while on earth He was only a man, and that He died as a man, that now He is an exalted spirit. Here are Pastor Russell's own words: "Our Redeemer existed as a spirit being before he was made flesh—he was chief of the angels—he was known as the Archangel, Michael, God's representative, the highest of all Jehovah's creation—he was the first creation of God." *Studies in the Scriptures*, Vol. V. p. 84, Ed. 1912.

"According to Scripture," writes Dr. Ironside, "Christ Jesus is God from all eternity, the ever-living uncreated Word (John 1: 1), whose glorious title is the Son, the Creator of the world and all things, who upholds all that exists (John 1: 3, 10; Col. 1: 13–17; Heb. 1: 1–3)." By this test all cults stand or fall. " 'What think ye of Christ?' is the test to try both your state and your scheme; you cannot be right in the rest, unless you think rightly of Him."

For nearly two thousand years the Church Universal has believed that the Scriptures affirm the deity of Jesus Christ; only the false cults have ever denied it. Having existed from all eternity, and having all the attributes of God, His claim to deity cannot be refuted.

He knew all things—past, present and future; where He came from, where He was going, His appointed hour, how He would suffer and die and when He would rise again. He was never confused or cornered and He could conceal Himself and escape at will. He accepted worship and forgave sins. Only of God could all this be true.

In numerous passages Jesus is called the Son of God, and in each instance it is a claim to deity. That the Jews so understood it, is proved by the fact that they accused Him of blasphemy and declared Him to be worthy of death. As the son of a king partakes of royal blood, so the Son of God partakes of deity. He was the unique and only begotten Son of God, born not of Joseph, but of the Holy Ghost, and being virgin born He was God the Son as no one else ever can be. If He was the son of an earthly father, then He was not the Son of God.

I have set forth the teaching of the Bible on "The Deity of Jesus Christ," in my book *The Battle for Truth,* and I challenge the false cults to answer my arguments. All they can do is to explain away the passages I have quoted; they dare not take them as they read. They may twist the Scriptures and interpret them to suit themselves, but they can never change what God has said. If they are honest they will bow in worship and exclaim with Thomas, "My Lord and my God."

I do not have to prove the deity of Christ; it is up to the unbeliever to disprove it, and that he can never do. I challenge him to answer the notes in the Scofield Reference Bible on John 20: 28. There he will find what the Book itself has to say about it.

2. *They deny the physical resurrection of Christ*

"Whether the body was dissolved into gases or whether it was still preserved somewhere . . . no one knows; nor is such knowledge necessary." *Studies in the Scriptures,* Vol. II, pp. 129, 130.

But Jesus said, "Behold my hands and my feet, that it is I myself; handle me and see; for a spirit hath not flesh and bones as ye see me have" (Luke 24: 39).

"Reach hither thy finger," He said to Thomas, "and behold my hands; and reach hither thy hand, and thrust it into my side: and be not faithless but believing" (John 20: 27).

Nothing further need be said. There is no suggestion of anything but a bodily resurrection. The tomb was empty. If we reject the physical resurrection of Christ we will have to destroy the whole of the New Testament. If we insist that it was the spirit and not the body that rose, then there was no resurrection, for the spirit does not die.

3. *They claim that Christ came in* 1874, *and that the age ended in* 1914

"1874 . . . when Christ the Bridegroom and Reaper actually came." *Studies in the Scriptures,* Vol. II, p. 240. "With the end of 1914, what God calls Babylon and what men call Christendom will have passed away." Id., p. 234. This is their teaching.

If so, then none of the prophecies were fulfilled, and there is no millennium yet. Acts 1: 11 and 1 Thess. 4: 17, 18 must be fulfilled when Christ returns. They have not yet been fulfilled, hence He has not yet come.

4. *They believe in soul sleep and teach that the grave is all the hell there is*

"Hell is the grave"—*Watchtower*. "Those who die are never again conscious"—*The Harp of God*, p. 45.

"Man does not have a soul separate and distinct from his body"—*Watchtower*.

But Ecclesiastes 12: 7 and Acts 2: 31 say he has. Our Lord's body went to one place, His soul to another. So the grave to which the body goes is not hades, hell or paradise to which the soul goes.

Luke 16: 19–31 forever settles the question of soul sleep. Hence they call it a parable and then invent a symbolic interpretation to defend their position, for all the characters are alive and conscious after death. I dare them to take it as it reads. And remember, it is not Gehenna, the final hell. See also Matthew 25: 41, 46.

The word "hell" (Gehenna) is used twelve times in the New Testament, and in every instance but one it is used by Jesus Christ Himself. So there is a hell in spite of what Jehovah's Witnesses say, and it is pictured as a lake of fire.

Practically all their quotations are from the old Testament. For instance, they quote the opinion of the writer of Ecclesiastes who wrote only of what he saw "under the sun". Everything above the sun was beyond his knowledge. Hence they use Ecclesiastes 3: 19–20, which speaks of the body only, but they ignore the twenty-first verse, which refers to the soul.

Then they quote Ecclesiastes 9: 10 as if it were the Word of God. These reasonings of man are set down by inspiration just as the false words of Satan are. But we must always distinguish between man's opinion and "Thus saith the Lord".

Then, too, they quote Psalm 6: 5. But who among the unsaved would remember God or give Him thanks? And

as for the righteous, how can they render God the service
they rendered on earth when in the body? The word is
not "remember" but "memorial" or service.

All such passages as Revelation 14: 10–11 and Revelation 20: 10, they must interpret symbolically; they dare
not take them as they read, and so they explain them as
"the perpetual captivity of death". Nonsense! How do
they know that their explanation is the right one? They
don't, but they have no choice, for such verses contradict
everything they teach.

The Bible tells us that those who have died are alive
and conscious; the dead do not sleep.

"So great a crowd of witnesses" (Heb. 12: 1). Who are
they? Why, they are the heroes of faith in chapter eleven.
Are they asleep, then? Not if they are watching us as we
run the Christian race. Not if they are witnesses.

Abraham, Samuel, Moses and the martyrs of Revelation were all alive, active, and conscious after death.

Paul, in 2 Corinthians 5: 8, says: "Absent from the
body, present with the Lord", and since our Lord is alive
and conscious, we, too, will be.

In Philippians 1: 23, he says: ". . . to depart, and to
be with Christ . . . is far better." Is it better to depart and
be unconscious? No, it is better to be with Him for we
will be as He is.

In Luke 23: 43, Jesus said: "Today shalt thou be with
me in paradise." How would the thief know he was in
paradise with Christ if he were unconscious? Jehovah's
Witnesses dare not take this statement as it reads. They
are compelled to change the punctuation and explain it
away.

"Blessed [happy] are the dead" (Rev. 14: 13). How
can they be happy—or miserable—if they are unconscious, or asleep? One has to be awake and conscious
to experience happiness.

In Isaiah 14: 9–11, the dead are moved, stirred up—
they speak. How then can they be unconscious; how can
they be asleep?

Revelation 6: 9–12 states that the dead cry with loud

voices. Then they must be awake. Certainly they are not
unconscious. Abraham rejoiced and was glad (John 8: 56).

"I am the God of Abraham, and the God of Isaac, and
the God of Jacob," said Jesus, "God is not the God of the
dead, but of the living" (Matt. 22: 32). He is the God
of those who are alive and know it.

My article, "Man's Future Destiny," chapter 7, in my
book *The Voice of Prophecy,* presents the teaching of the
Bible on this subject and I challenge the false cults to
answer it.

5. *They hold out no assurance of a present salvation but
claim there will be an opportunity to be saved after
death*

"The 'ransom for all' given by 'the man Christ Jesus'
does not guarantee everlasting life or blessing for any
man; but it does guarantee to every man another opportunity or trial for life everlasting." *Studies in the Scriptures,* Vol. I, p. 150. So say Jehovah's Witnesses.

Yet they produce no proof, for there is none. They
quote Jeremiah 31: 15–17, but it has no bearing whatever
on the subject. I challenge them to produce a single clear-
cut New Testament statement.

Most certainly the rich man in Luke 16 had no second
chance, but to disprove it they invent a symbolic interpretation.

God says, "Now is the accepted time; behold, NOW is
the day of salvation" (2 Cor. 6: 2). He holds out no offer
for the future.

It is clear that present salvation only is available. He
that believeth HATH everlasting life (John 3: 36, John
5: 24). "He that hath the Son HATH life" (1 John 5: 12).
"Ye may know that ye HAVE eternal life" (1 John 5: 13).
It is always a present possession.

6. *They know nothing of the New Testament experiences
of conversion, regeneration or the new birth*

The words "faith" and "believe" are not in their vocab-
ulary. Life with them is based on obedience; namely,

works; and in none of their books do they tell a sinner how to be saved *now*.

May I suggest that they study carefully the Gospel of John, and that then they open their hearts to the Lord Jesus Christ and accept Him as their Saviour here and now, for there will be no chance hereafter.

"These are written, that ye might believe that Jesus is the Christ, the Son of God; and that believing ye might have life through his name" (John 20: 31).

"Except a man be born again," Jesus says, "he cannot see the Kingdom of God" (John 3: 3). Have Jehovah's Witnesses been born again? If so, when, where, how? They know they have not, for they do not believe in the New Birth; therefore they do not believe God's Word. And "except a man be born again, he cannot see the Kingdom of God".

CHAPTER XIV

WHO ARE THE SEVENTH-DAY ADVENTISTS AND WHAT DO THEY TEACH?

LIKE Christian Science, Theosophy and Spiritism, Seventh-Day Adventism was founded by a woman, Mrs. Ellen G. White, about A.D. 1860.

It is classed as a False Cult because of its unscriptural teachings.

1. *It denies Christ's sinlessness*

"In His humanity Christ partook of our sinful, fallen nature," it says. "On His human side, Christ inherited just what every child of Adam inherits—a sinful nature." (*Desire of Ages*, p. 24). "In His veins was the incubus of a tainted heredity . . . , bad blood and inherited meanness" (*Signs of the Times*, March 1927).

So says Seventh-Day Adventism. But what say the Scriptures? "In him is no sin" (1 John 3: 5). See Hebrews 4: 15; 1 Peter 2: 22.

2. *It denies the Biblical doctrine of the atoning sacrifice of Christ as the only means of man's salvation, and teaches that "the scapegoat typified Satan, the author of sin, upon whom the sins of the truly penitent will finally be placed"*

So says Seventh-Day Adventism. What blasphemy! For the Scriptures again and again declare that Christ, and Christ alone, bore our sins. This is "another gospel" that Paul never preached. Where in the whole of the New Testament is there a verse that mentions Satan as our sin-bearer? I challenge the Adventists to find one.

3. *It teaches that "Christ came to the Heavenly sanctuary in 1844, to complete the work of atonement and to carry out an investigative judgment," since the sins of believers, it claims, "are still on the books of record"*

"We dissent from the view that the atonement was made upon the cross, as is generally held," are their very words of denial of this greatest of all Bible truths. Again: "The blood of Christ . . . was not to cancel sin." Mrs. White taught that since 1814 Christ has been atoning for our sins. Here are her words: "We are now living in the great day of atonement." Again, "Christ did not make the atonement when He shed His blood upon the cross", and, "It is impossible to conclude that a complete work of atoning for sin was wrought upon the cross" (*Looking Unto Jesus*, p. 237).

So says Seventh-Day Adventism. But what say the Scriptures? "It is finished" (John 19: 30). Again and again we are assured that our sins are remembered no more. Every passage speaks of a completed work. The Bible says, "he offered one sacrifice for sins forever". See Galatians 3: 13; Hebrews 1: 3; 9: 11–12, 26; 10: 12–14.

4. *Like Jehovah's Witnesses, another false cult, it denies eternal punishment and teaches soul-sleep*

"The theory of eternal punishment is one of the false doctrines that constitute the wine of the abomination of Babylon," it says. "Sin and sinners will be blotted out of existence"—Spicer. "The state to which we are reduced by death is one of silence, inactivity and entire unconsciousness. Between death and resurrection the dead sleep."—Spicer. But since I have completely answered this denial in my article "Who Are Jehovah's Witnesses and What Do They Teach?" I will not repeat what I have said here.

5. *It places the believer under the Mosaic Law instead of under grace, insisting, among other things, on abstinence from the eating of pork, rabbit, lobster, crab, oysters—and the observance of Saturday, the Jewish Sabbath, instead of Sunday*

(1) *The Law*

Let me say that no Gentile was ever told to keep the law, unless he first became a proselyte. Nor was the law ever given to the Church; it was given to Israel and to no other nation or people.

Moreover, the law, written on stone, "the ministration of death", was fulfilled and abolished, and the ministration of the Spirit substituted (2 Cor. 3: 7–13). Compare Romans 3: 20–21, 24–28; 4: 9–17; 10: 5; 11: 6; Galatians 2: 15–16, 19, 21; 3: 10–12, 19, 21, 24–25; 4: 8–10.

Paul wrote the Epistle to the Galatians for the one purpose of separating law from grace. No man can read it prayerfully and remain under the law. Jewish teachers had mixed law with grace. Hence Paul's exclamation in Galatians 1: 6. Hence also Paul's terrible rebuke of Peter in Galatians 2: 11–16. Paul says he is "dead to the law" (Gal. 2: 19). And in Galations 2: 21 he states that righteousness cannot come by the law. If so, Christ died in vain. The law is purely of works and never of faith (Gal. 3: 12).

The law, declares Paul in Galatians 3: 19, was given only until Christ. It but conducts us to Him that our justification may be purely by faith (Gal. 3: 24). Like a mirror, the law reveals our true state, shows us our sin, but, just as we cannot use the mirror to wash with, so we cannot use the law for our cleansing. Christ's blood alone is sufficient.

Then Galatians 3: 25 settles it forever, by definitely declaring, in spite of what man says, that "we are no longer under a schoolmaster". God help us to believe it lest we sin a great sin. We are no longer under law. Hence Paul asks, "How turn ye again to the weak and beggarly elements, whereunto ye desire again to be in bondage? Ye observe days, and months, and times, and years" (Gal. 4: 9, 10). Yes, days—sabbaths. Why? And again, "Whosoever of you are justified by the law; ye are fallen from grace" (Gal. 5: 4).

Read the verdict of the apostles in Acts 15: 19–24. And this decision, remember, was rendered by the Church at Jerusalem. Certain teachers had told the Gentiles that, unless they were circumcised and kept the law of Moses, they could not be saved. The Apostles said, "We gave no such commandment." How about it, my friend? Had you not better read once again Acts, chapter 15?

But, someone may inquire, did not Christ Himself keep the law? Yes, He did, always emphasizing, however, the spirit rather than the letter. But you must remember that Jesus was a Jew, born under the law, and that the law was not fulfilled until He paid the price of man's redemption on the cross and became Himself the Sin-Offering, our Sacrifice, God's Lamb. It was then He cried "Finished". So that, as a Jew, He kept the law until He fulfilled it on Calvary; then He ushered in the new dispensation, the day of grace.

Now let me give you the New Testament fulfilment of the law: "All the law is fulfilled in one word, even in this, Thou shalt love thy neighbour as thyself" (Gal. 5: 14). Do you? You cannot be saved by law and grace; you must be saved by grace and grace alone. Not your works of obedience, but Christ's meritorious death.

The moral law and the injunctions of the Epistles you will gladly, joyfully carry out, not as a matter of duty, but because you are a new creature in Christ; and the Holy Spirit within will work out through your life the law of love, which will exclude unrighteousness and result in a holy walk with God. But from all Jewish and Mosaic ceremonial laws you are forever free.

Oh that you would study and believe Galatians, and thus enjoy your liberty in Christ. I challenge you to read it. For if you do, if you accept its plain and definite statements, you will never again be in bondage to Jewish law. It is Paul's epistle to the Seventh-Day Adventists. And you will learn from it, as stated in Romans 10: 4, that "Christ is the end of the law".

(2) *Food*

"God has forbidden the use of pork, rabbits, lobsters, crabs, oysters. Those who are using such foods will be destroyed" (*Belief*, pp. 22, 23).

So says Seventh-Day Adventism. But where, I ask, have such foods been forbidden? Certainly not in the New Testament, and Church doctrine is found only in the Scriptures after Pentecost; never before.

Paul tells us to eat what is set before us, asking no questions (I Cor. 10: 27). "Let no man, therefore, judge you in meat or in drink," he says (Col. 2: 16). And he warns us of Seventh-Day Adventists and others who would command us "to abstain from meats which God hath created to be received with thanksgiving" (I Tim. 4: 1–5).

(3) *The Sabbath*

In discussing this question we cannot use the Old Testament except for example and precept. Church doctrine is found only in the Scriptures written after Pentecost. God commanded Israel to do many things that He never told the Church to do. Our sole authority therefore must be the New Testament, especially the Acts and the Epistles. We cannot take the instructions given to the Jews and apply them to the Church. Never confuse the Commandments of Jesus with the commandments of Moses.

1. In the whole of the New Testament there is no command to keep the Sabbath. All the other nine are repeated again and again, but the Sabbath commandment is not even mentioned. In enumerating the commandments to the rich young ruler, Jesus never even referred to the Sabbath (Luke 18: 20). Where is the Sabbath mentioned in the commandments of Romans 13: 9? Sabbath-breaking is never designated a sin in the New Testament Scriptures. Jesus did not command His disciples to keep the Sabbath. In fact the Jews tried to kill Him because He Himself had broken it (John 5: 16–18), they said.

2. The Council at Jerusalem never even mentioned the Sabbath when telling Gentile converts what to do (Acts 15: 19–29). The Epistles of Hebrews and James written to converted Israelites, make no reference whatever to the Sabbath. And Paul never hints at Sabbath-keeping in any of his letters. Why then do the Seventh-Day Adventists insist on keeping it?

3. The word *Sabbath* occurs for the first time in Exodus 16: 23. For over 2,000 years after the Fall there was no mention of it. There is no record that the patriarchs ever heard of it. In Nehemiah 9: 13–14, we have the state-

ment, "Thou madest known unto them thy holy sabbath", and in Ezekiel 20: 12 "I gave them my sabbaths". Both these announcements refer to the days of Moses. This was something entirely new (Deut. 5: 15). In Genesis 2: 1–3 it states that God rested on the seventh day, but it was not then called the Sabbath. Adam was never told to keep it.

4. Let me state very emphatically that the Seventh-Day Adventists did not start keeping the Sabbath because of anything the Bible has to say about it. Don't let them deceive you. Their arguments were not based on the Word of God. Even Mrs. White, their founder, did not believe that the fourth commandment was binding. Her observance of the Sabbath, as well as her followers', was based purely and wholly on a supposed revelation she is reputed to have had. She speaks of it as a vision in which she saw the fourth commandment encircled by a halo of light, and it was only after that experience that she taught that it must be observed. Think of basing a doctrine on a vision.

5. Sabbath observance was a ceremonial law. Moral law is for everyone. All know right and wrong, even the heathen. But no one could possibly know which day to keep until God revealed it. The same is true of tithing, circumcision and eating. These ceremonial laws show that the Israelites were set apart (sanctified) from all other nations (Exod. 31: 12–13). Now all ceremonial law was fulfilled in Christ and abolished, namely, eating (1 Tim. 4: 4–5), circumcision (1 Cor. 7: 18), and Sabbath-keeping (Col. 2: 16–17). We are even warned against Sabbath-keeping in the New Testament. "Let no man judge you in respect of the sabbath days" (Col. 2: 16–17). Why then do the Seventh-Day Adventists pass judgment on those who do not keep it? Paul urges a complete break with Judaism along these lines. In Galatians 4: 10–11, he says: "Ye observe days . . . I am afraid of you." In any case we are not saved by keeping the law, either moral or ceremonial, but by trusting Christ. Works are but the evidence of salvation.

6. According to Hebrews 8: 13, the old covenant van-

ished away. "The ministration of death, written and engraved in stones," was abolished by Jesus Christ (2 Cor. 3: 7–16). Not, mark you, as the Seventh-Day Adventists state, by Constantine, but by Christ. He came not to destroy but to fulfil, and He fulfilled. Our Sabbath is Christ.

7. The Bible says nothing about Sunday observance being the mark of the Beast, or that those who do not keep Saturday will be lost, as Seventh-Day Adventists state. The Pope did not change the Sabbath from Saturday to Sunday. The Council of Laodicia merely stated that it was not binding on Christians. Long before then the Church observed the first day. Saturday has always been the seventh day, and Exodus 20: 10 says: "But the seventh day is the sabbath of the Lord thy God." Saturday is therefore the Jewish Sabbath. Sunday is not the Sabbath. Sunday is the Lord's Day. The Sabbath day has never been changed. "Why then," ask the Adventists, "did Paul go to the Synagogue on the Sabbath Day?" Simply because he went where the people were. It was in the synagogue they congregated and it was on the Sabbath, and it was there he could give them the Gospel.

8. We are not commanded to keep Sunday. We do so willingly. First because it commemorates the resurrection of our Lord. Second, because God commands us to meet together, and since the early Christians met on the first day we follow their example (Heb. 10: 25, Acts 20: 7). Why did they not meet on the Sabbath? Third, because John worshipped on that day, and so do we. The Sabbath was only for rest. Fourth, in 1 Corinthians 16: 2 the first day is mentioned as a day for offerings. Hence the entire Christian Church has always recognized Sunday as the Lord's Day.

9. On the Sabbath no burden could be carried (Jer. 17: 21), no fire kindled (Exod. 35: 3), and no cooking done (Exod. 16: 23). This could only apply locally in a land where the people could live without heat. It would be impossible in the Arctic. The penalty for doing these

things which broke the Sabbath, was death (Num. 15: 32–36). Who keeps it today? Certainly not the Seventh-Day Adventists. There can be no half-way measure or the Sabbath is broken after all. If the Jewish Sabbath, Saturday, is to be kept at all, it must be kept exactly as commanded. And God forbade even the collecting of a bundle of sticks with which to kindle a fire on the Sabbath Day (Exod. 35: 3). The Sabbath was given to one nation only, namely—Israel. No Gentile was ever commanded to keep it. But, you argue, the Sabbath was given long before Moses. And my answer is, so was circumcision (Gen. 17, Rom. 4: 9–13). Why, then, do you accept the one and reject the other?

10. According to Barnabas (A.D. 100), Ignatius (A.D. 107), Martyr (A.D. 145), Irenaeus (A.D. 155), Tertullian (A.D. 200), Eusebius (A.D. 315) etc., Christians repudiated the seventh day and recognized the first day, and that long before there was a Pope. Here are their statements:

"We keep the eighth day. No longer . . . the Sabbath, but . . . the Lord's Day. Sunday is the day . . . because it is the first day of the week. On the Lord's own day gather yourselves together. We keep the Lord's Day, the day on which Jesus rose from the dead. No longer observing sabbaths. Sunday is the day upon which we all hold our assembly. Jesus Christ on that day rose from the dead. On that day called Sunday all gather together. On the first day of the week we assemble ourselves together. The observance of the Sabbath is demonstrated to have been temporary. We solemnize the day after Saturday, the day of our Lord's resurrection. The churches throughout the world observe the practice that has prevailed from apostolic tradition—the Lord's Day."

Hence, the Lord's Day was kept universally right from the days of the apostles; and this practice was never changed until a woman, Mrs. Ellen G. White, and her followers, the Seventh-Day Adventists, changed it less than a hundred years ago. What audacity! Has the whole

Christian Church been wrong for the past nineteen centuries, and the Seventh-Day Adventists alone right? Does Mrs. White know more than Paul, the Church fathers and all the Christian theologians of the last two thousand years? Preposterous!

11. D. M. Canright (1830–1919) held the highest positions in the Seventh-Day Adventist movement. He was well acquainted with its leaders, including Ellen G. White. His book (418 pages) is the outstanding work explaining the unscriptural positions of Seventh-Day legalism. Once he was honoured; today he is repudiated because of his unanswerable exposure. This is what he says:

"After keeping the Seventh Day for twenty-eight years; after having persuaded more than a thousand others to keep it; after having read my Bible through, verse by verse, more than twenty times; after having scrutinized to the best of my ability every text, line and word in the whole Bible having the remotest bearing upon the Sabbath question; after having looked up all these, both in the original and in many translations; after having searched in lexicons, concordances, commentaries and dictionaries; after having read arm-fuls of books on both sides of the question; after having read every line in all the early church fathers upon this point; after having written several works in favour of the Seventh Day, which were satisfactory to my brethren: after having debated the question more than a dozen times; after seeing the fruits of keeping it; and after weighing all the evidence in the fear of God, and of the judgment day, I am fully settled in my own mind and conscience that *the evidence is against the keeping of the Seventh Day.*"

Salvation Unknown

Seventh-Day Adventists are not out to win new converts from among the unsaved; their work is to proselytize. And whether at home or on the mission field, they labour among the converts of other workers, and strive to ensnare them in their delusions and heresies. They are blind leaders of the blind, living in bondage and slavery worse than death. And they often strive to hide their identity. Why, I wonder?

With the Seventh-Day Adventist there is no such thing as a present, know-so salvation. Theirs is a religion of works, for they believe that works as well as faith are essential to salvation. Here is their statement in their own words: "Seventh-Day Adventists teach that both faith and works are essential in salvation."

But works in the New Testament are always set forth as the evidence of salvation, and in scores of passages the statement is made that we are NOT saved by works, but only by faith. "Not of works lest any man should boast" (Eph. 2: 9). James speaks of works as the evidence or proof of faith. "I will show thee my faith by my works," he says (Jas. 2: 18).

In numerous verses we are taught that salvation is a present possession. "He that hath the Son HATH life" (1 John 5: 12). Moreover we can be sure that we are saved, "Ye may *know* that ye have eternal life," says John (1 John 5: 13).

There is no joy in Seventh-Day Adventism. It is a religion of fear and uncertainty. I would urge its victims to turn from the visions and false teachings of its erratic founder to the freedom of the glorious Gospel of our Lord and Saviour Jesus Christ.

CHAPTER XV

WHO ARE THE CHRISTIAN SCIENTISTS AND WHAT DO THEY TEACH?

LIKE Seventh-Day Adventism, Theosophy and Spiritism, Christian Science was founded by a woman, Mary Baker Glover Patterson Eddy, who got it from Dr. P. P. Quimby, notwithstanding the denial by the Circuit Court in 1883. She had three husbands.

It claims that its text book is inspired, yet it has been changed again and again. Compare the 1893 edition with the 1909.

It uses Bible terms, but it attaches an entirely different meaning to them.

First, it is not scientific

It denies the reality of sickness and matter, therefore it is not scientific.

Speaking of a burning ship, it declares that "the catastrophe never occurred except in the imagination of the people". What an absurdity! A fact of history, a fearful tragedy, witnessed by thousands, is construed as a false report.

It says you are only as heavy as you think you are. Do scales think? Nonsense!

Milk, it declares, would be as intoxicating as whisky if we only thought so. What an imagination! Can a scientist so think as to get drunk on milk? Why does whisky and not milk make calves drunk? What unscientific nonsense!

Tuberculosis and all diseases are but "images of mental thought," it says. Then why do animals get sick, and why do people contract contagious diseases when their minds are unconscious of the fact that there are any around? Absurd!

103

"Heat and cold are products of the mind," it contends. Then what lowers and raises the thermometer? Do thermometers have brains? Scientific? Where is their intelligence?

"Food neither strengthens nor weakens the body", it maintains. But the fact is, it does. Even a practitioner learns that.

If mortal mind says "I am deaf and blind", it will be so, declares Christian Science. Well, has a Christian Scientist ever done it? I challenge him to try. What fools!

"Bones are only the substance of thought", it insists. What then if a Christian Scientist falls from a high building? Can he so think that his bones will not be broken? Let him try. Crazy, isn't it?

Christian Science says "there is no death". Then we are savages because we bury people alive.

I say it is not scientific, for it contradicts every known law of true science. And because it is not scientific, it heals nobody except those whose sickness is mental or imaginary; at best it is nothing but mind over matter. More than ninety per cent of sick people get well in any case. Nature sees to that. Many of these genuinely sick ultimately die of the very disease of which they were supposed to have been healed by Christian Science.

Second, it is not Christian

It denies the great doctrines of the Bible, therefore it is not Christian.

1. It denies the personality of God and the reality of Satan

Let me quote it verbatim. "What is Mind? Mind is god. The principle of Divine metaphysics is god. Life, Truth, and Love constitute god."

"A lie is all the devil there is."

I do not have to state that the Bible in hundreds of places speaks of a personal God and a personal devil, and refers to God as a Father.

2. *It denies the Bible doctrine of the incarnation*

"Mary's conception was spiritual," it says. "The virgin mother conceived this idea of God, and gave to her idea the name of Jesus."

But the Bible says, "Every spirit that confesseth that Jesus Christ is come in the flesh, is of God: and every spirit that confesseth not that Jesus Christ is come in the flesh, is not of God" (1 John 4: 2, 3).

3. *It denies the deity of Jesus*

"Jesus was a good man," it says. In other words, He was not God. Merely "a good man", F. W. Boorer writes, "Your statement that Christian Science denies the deity of Jesus is correct."

"According to Scripture," writes Dr. Ironside, "Christ Jesus is God from all eternity, the ever-living uncreated Word (John 1: 1), whose glorious title is the Son, the Creator of the world and all things, who upholds all that exists" (John 1: 3, 10; Col. 1: 13–17; Heb. 1: 1–3). By this test all cults stand or fall. " 'What think ye of Christ?' is the test to try both your state and your scheme: you cannot be right in the rest, unless you think rightly of Him."

For nearly 2,000 years the Church Universal has believed that the Scriptures affirm the deity of Jesus Christ; only the false cults have ever denied it. Having existed from all eternity, and having all the attributes of God, His claim to deity cannot be refuted.

He knew all things—past, present and future; where He came from, where He was going, His appointed hour, how He would suffer and die and when He would rise again. He was never confused or cornered and He could conceal Himself and escape at will. He accepted worship and forgave sins. Only of God could all this be true.

In numerous passages Jesus is called the Son of God, and in each instance it is a claim to deity. That the Jews so understood it is proved by the fact that they accused Him of blasphemy and declared Him to be worthy of death. As the son of a king partakes of royal blood, so the Son of God partakes of deity. He was the unique and only begotten Son of God, born not of Joseph, but of the Holy Ghost, and being virgin born He was the Son as no one else ever can be. If He was the son of an earthly father, then He was not the Son of God.

I have set forth the teachings of the Bible on "The Deity of Jesus Christ," in my book, *The Battle for Truth,* and I challenge the false cults to answer my arguments. All they can do is to explain away the passages I have quoted; they dare not take them as they read. They may twist the Scriptures and interpret them to suit themselves, but they can never change what God has said. If they are honest they will bow in worship and exclaim with Thomas, "My Lord and my God."

I do not have to prove the deity of Christ; it is up to the unbeliever to disprove it, and that he can never do. I challenge him to answer the notes in the Scofield Reference Bible on John 20: 28. There he will find what the Book itself has to say about it.

4. *It claims that Jesus never died, rose, or ascended*

"Pitying friends took down from the cross the fainting form of Jesus and buried it out of their sight," it explains.

"His disciples believed Jesus to be dead, while He was hidden in the sepulchre, whereas He was alive," it reveals.

"Jesus' students . . . learned that He had not died," it declares.

Wonderful! What a revelation! But where did Mrs. Eddy get it? Certainly not from the Bible. Scores upon scores of passages tell us that He died, rose and ascended. Who is Mrs. Eddy to deny it?

5. *It denies the efficacy of prayer*

"Petitioning a personal deity . . . cannot be beneficial," it tells us. Then it continues: "Prayer to a personal God is a hindrance. God is not influenced by man."

Yet the Bible simply abounds with exhortations to pray to a personal God who is spoken of as our heavenly

Father, and with numerous incidents of answered prayer. Which are we to believe?

Isn't it strange that their practitioners collect substantial money for prayer-treatment, when they do not believe it to be beneficial or that money is real?

6. *It denies the reality of sin*

"Sin is an error of mortal mind: evil is but an illusion," it says. "Man is incapable of sin."

But the Bible states that "If we say we have no sin we deceive ourselves, and the truth is not in us" (I John I: 8). How different! The man who believes that sin is an error and evil an illusion is liable to be guilty of anything. I certainly wouldn't want to trust him very far. If "man is incapable of sin", then why does the Bible say "all have sinned"?

7. *It repudiates the atonement*

Christian Scientists say that they do not believe in "pinning one's faith without works to another's vicarious efforts". And that "Jesus never ransomed man by paying the debt that sin incurs".

Can you believe it! Why, that is exactly what the Bible does teach. "Christ Jesus . . . gave Himself *a ransom* for all" (I Tim. 2: 5–6). "Christ died for our sins" (I Cor. 15: 3). "Who his own self bare our sins in his own body on the tree" (I Pet. 2: 24). "The Lord hath laid on him the iniquity of us all" (Isa. 53: 6). There are literally scores of passages that tell us that Christ's death was vicarious, that He became a ransom for us, that He, and He alone, paid our debt of sin, and that He is our one and only hope of salvation.

Christian Science says: "One sacrifice, however great, is insufficient to pay for the debt of sin. The material blood of Jesus was no more efficacious to cleanse from sin when it was shed upon the accursed tree, than when it was flowing in his veins." What blasphemy! In a hundred places the Bible teaches the very opposite. "Without SHEDDING of blood is no remission" (Heb. 9: 22).

"Once . . . hath he appeared to put away sin by the sacrifice of himself" (Heb. 9: 26). So ONE sacrifice *is* sufficient.

8. *It denies that men are lost and need a Saviour*

"There is no human soul that sins and is spiritually lost," it declares. Whereas Jesus said, "The Son of man is come to seek and to save that which was lost" (Luke 19: 10). Who are we to believe, Mrs. Eddy or Jesus?

9. *It declares that the Bible contains "error, myths, fables, legends, untrue history and even lies"*

There, now you have it. No wonder their doctrines are false, they have no authority. The Bible to them is not the infallible Word of God. Hence they have manufactured a bible of their own. No wonder their system is neither scientific nor Christian. How could it be?

Christian Scientists know absolutely nothing of conversion, regeneration, or the New Birth. Therefore they are not Christians, for they have never been saved. I would point them to "the Lamb of God which taketh away the sin of the world" (John 1: 29). I would direct them to Isaiah 53: 5–6 and to John 1: 12; 3: 14–18, 36; 5: 24. Also 1 John 5: 11–12. May they then turn away from "science falsely so called" (1 Tim. 6: 20), and receive Jesus Christ as a personal Saviour, lest they incur the wrath of God and perish in their sin.

CHAPTER XVI

WHO ARE THE MORMONS AND WHAT DO THEY TEACH?

MORMONISM started with six people in a house in the State of New York, on April 6, 1830. It was founded by Joseph Smith, who was known as a notorious liar, vulgar in speech, and immoral. In 1844 he and his brother were arrested and imprisoned, and on June 27 a mob broke into the jail and lynched them both.

Smith manufactured the Mormon Bible known as the Book of Mormon. A novel was left by Solomon Spalding in Patterson's Printing Office at Pittsburg. Sidney Regdon found it and with Joseph Smith's help, he invented a story about gold plates and spectacles. Smith professed to translate it and thus we have the Mormon Bible.

Joseph Smith was succeeded by Brigham Young who, in 1846, led the Mormons to Utah, where they bound themselves by secret oaths, offered human sacrifices, made blood atonements, and committed murder. On September 9, 1857, a group of California emigrants were massacred (so it is reported) by the Mormons under the leadership of John D. Lee who, seventeen years later was executed for the crime. Young died August 29, 1877, leaving an estate of over two million dollars, twenty-five wives, and fifty-six children.

Such is a brief excerpt from the history of Mormonism as recorded in the *Encyclopædia Britannica,* Eleventh Edition, 1911, Vol. XVIII, pages 842–8.

Mormonism is designated a false cult because its beliefs are pagan and unscriptural, and its practices anti-Christian. Worldliness characterizes its gatherings, it authorizes dancing on its church premises and thus makes its appeal to the flesh.

The Reorganized Church of Latter Day Saints is no different at all except that it finally repudiated polygamy and rejected the Adam-god doctrine of the Brighamites. But when the break came, 20,000 went with polygamous Young, and only 1,000 with the Josephites. Brodie claims that Joseph Smith himself had forty-eight wives. He it was who wrote the "Revelation on Celestial Marriage."

1. The Mormons do not believe there is a verse in our Bible that conveys the exact sense of the original, and yet they quote thousands of verses verbatim from the Bible in their Book of Mormon.

2. They believe in Polytheism; namely, many gods, and that the gods have material bodies just as we have. "The Father has a body of flesh and bones as tangible as man's."—Joseph Smith. But the Bible says, "God is a Spirit" (John 4: 24).

3. They believe that Adam is the god of this world, and the only god with whom we have to do, and that Eve was one of his wives. Here are their own words: "When our father Adam came into the garden of Eden, he came into it with a celestial body, and brought Eve, one of his wives, with him. He helped to make and organize this world. He is our father and our God, and the only God with whom we have to do."—Brigham Young.

4. They believe that the gods generate children just as men do.

5. They teach that Jesus Christ was the natural offspring of Adam and Mary, and not that He was begotten by the Holy Spirit. Again I quote: "When the Virgin Mary conceived the child Jesus, the Father had begotten him in his own likeness. He was NOT begotten by the Holy Ghost. And who was the Father? He was the first of the human family. Jesus, our elder brother, was begotten in the flesh by the same character that was in the garden of Eden and who is our Father in Heaven."—Brigham Young.

6. They believe in polygamy even though the Book of Mormon definitely forbids it, Joseph Smith having received a special revelation in 1843, so they say, authorizing it.

"Abraham received concubines and they bare him children, and it was accounted unto him for righteousness. Go ye therefore and do the works of Abraham, enter ye into my law, and ye shall be saved. But if ye enter not into my law [of polygamy] ye cannot receive the promise of my father, which he made unto Abraham."—Joseph Smith.

They believe that Jesus was a polygamist. "Jesus Christ was a polygamist; Mary and Martha, the sisters of Lazarus, were his plural wives, and Mary Magdalene was another. The bridal feast at Cana . . . was on the occasion of one of his own marriages."—Brigham Young.

7. They teach that man, if faithful to Mormonism, is to become a god, creating and governing worlds and peopling them with his own offspring. Here again is their own statement: "They shall be gods, creating and governing worlds, and peopling them with their offspring. What God was once, we are now; what God is now, we shall be."

8. They believe that a man's wife will continue to bear him children in the world to come, and that it is therefore his solemn duty to practise polygamy. I quote them verbatim: "A man's wife will continue to bear him children in the world to come. Hence it is his duty to be a polygamist. Child-bearing is to be the chief business of woman during the eternal ages."

9. They teach that the Holy Spirit is a "divine fluid", an impersonal energy or cosmic force.

10. They believe in a "second chance", and practise baptism for the dead. "Millions of earth's sons and daughters have passed out of the body without obeying the law of baptism. Many of them will gladly accept the word and law of the Lord when it is proclaimed to them in the spirit world. But they cannot there attend to ordinances that belong to the sphere which they have left. Can nothing be done in their case? . . . yes . . . The living may be baptized for the dead."—Penrose.

11. They do not believe in the great Bible doctrine of justification by faith. "The sectarian doctrine of justifica-

tion by faith alone has exercised an influence for evil since the early days of Christianity."—Talmadge.

12. They base forgiveness solely on obedience to the teachings of Mormonism, and they state that one must believe in Joseph Smith as a prophet and the Book of Mormon in order to be saved, the conditions of salvation being repentance, faith, baptism, laying on of the hands of Mormon elders, and obedience to the Mormon Church.

13. The Mormon Bible is not the Christian's Bible. It is not God's Word. Hence Mormons are not Christians. Their teachings and practices are utterly contrary to the Scriptures, and abhorrent to all clean-minded people. They know nothing of salvation through the finished work of Christ. I would refer those of them who want to be saved to such passages as Isaiah 53: 5–6, John 1: 12; 3: 15–18, 36; 5: 24, Acts 4: 12; 16: 30–31. Romans 4: 5; 6: 23, and may God open their eyes.

CHAPTER XVII

WHO ARE THE BRITISH-ISRAELITES AND WHAT DO THEY TEACH?

BRITISH-ISRAELISM claims that the Anglo-Saxon races, viz., Great Britain and the United States, constitute the lost ten tribes.

Origin and History

The first advocate of British-Israelism was Dr. Abadie —1723. He said that the ten tribes would be found in the British Isles.

The second advocate was Richard Brothers, a half-crazed British naval officer, who was born in the year 1789. He claimed to be "the nephew of God", and a descendant of King David. He predicted that the Jews would return to Palestine in his life time, and that he would become "the prince of the Hebrews" and world ruler. The authorities placed him in a lunatic asylum.

The third advocate was Edward Hine. In 1871 he wrote his book, *Identification of the British Nation with Lost Israel*. Edward Hine, who held many strange fallacies, claimed to be "the Deliverer out of Zion".

It remained, however, for John Wilson to put British-Israelism on its present basis. His book is entitled *Our Israelitish Origin*.

But John Wilson, contrary to Hine, included the Germans as Israelites. And it may be of interest to note here, that one of the leaders of British-Israelism on his visit to India, made this amazing statement: "This appeal is also to you, O brethren, who are yourselves Indians, but are verily also the sons of Jacob."

Stranger still, there has been a movement in Japan claiming that the Japanese as a nation are Israelites, and thereby disrupting missionary work on a large scale. A missionary from Japan tells me that the identifications are just as strong and just as convincing in favour of the Japanese being the lost tribes as they are that the Anglo-Saxon races are Israelites.

In view of the origin of the movement, can we be condemned for rejecting it? Men who would make the absurd statements that Richard Brothers and Edward Hine made, are surely untrustworthy as leaders and teachers.

Fact or Theory

The British-Israelites themselves admit that British-Israelism is only a theory, and while they are prepared to base their teachings on a mere theory, I am not.

For instance, Rev. John Wild, D.D., one of their most fervent adherents, makes the following statement: "This, you say, is *theory*. Grant it."

Bishop Titcombe, another of their advocates, has this to say: "Until a better *theory* can be propounded, it is worthy of our fullest belief."

Surely no scholar would talk like that. As a matter of fact that is the position taken by the atheistic scientists who endorse evolution. They know it is nothing but a *theory* and yet they expect their students to swallow it nevertheless. Some of us, however, want facts, not theories.

Their Two Bibles

British-Israelites claim that they stand for the Bible, the whole Bible, and that they believe it from cover to cover, and on that ground they cannot understand my attitude. But I would remind them of the fact the Christian Scientists and the Russellites make exactly the same claim. They insist that they accept the Bible, the whole Bible, and abide by its teachings. Hence, that argument is value-less. Mrs. Eddy and Judge Rutherford place their own interpretation on the Word of God. And while they claim to believe the Bible, they really do not. The same is true of British-Israelism.

The British-Israelites profess to have two Bibles. God's Word alone does not satisfy them. They would add to the Revelation already given. Their other Bible is the Great Pyramid of Egypt, upon which they have built the most fantastic theories imaginable.

It was my privilege when I was in Egypt to visit the Great Pyramid. I was taken all through the passage-ways and the various chambers, and I am very frank in saying that it has nothing whatever to do with prophecy, or God's programme for the future.

The conclusions at which the British-Israelites have arrived in regard to the Pyramid have had to be altered again and again. I know of nothing so utterly absurd and childish as the things they are saying in regard to what they dare to call their "other Bible".

No, my friends, there is but one Bible, the Word of God. It is absolutely authoritative and we need no other. Our doctrines must be based on God's revelation in the Scriptures, and not on the idle speculations of men.

They have no Answer

Some years ago a British-Israelite said that Edward would be Britain's last ruler. Now Great Britain has a queen. How does he explain it?

British-Israelites know but little of the truth. They are very one-sided. They think and write only in terms of their own fantastic theory. All Bible students and teachers, no matter how great, are discounted just because they cannot see the so-called truth of Anglo-Israelism. But a teacher who has little or no standing from a scholastic and theological position is recognized by them as a great Bible student if only he advocates their theory.

What the Encyclopædias Say

But now let us turn to the greatest of authorities, namely, the encyclopædias. Again and again they insist that only highly educated people with academic training are capable of dealing with British-Israel truth. In other words, it is not for the common people. They are considered incapable of understanding. How different to the ministry of our Lord. The common people heard Him gladly.

But now, if the British-Israelites really want the opinion of scholars, the greatest scholars and theologians, they are available. If they are really sincere in their statement that only the highly trained intelligentsia are capable of discussing the subject, then they will listen to what the encyclopædias have to say.

First of all, the *New International*. And this is what it says: "The theory is destitute of scientific proof."

Second, *American*. It is even stronger: "A peculiar belief untenable on any scientific grounds."

Third, *Chambers*: "A theory that sets at defiance all ethnological and linguistic evidence."

Last of all, and most important, the *Britannica*. And the *Britannica* speaks in no uncertain language: "The theory of Anglo-Israelism rests on premises which are deemed by scholars, both theological and anthropological, to be utterly unsound."

That should settle the question. To think of an ordinary individual stressing his opinion and insisting that he knows more than the great scholars, theological and anthropological, who have weighed the question and then had the verdict published in the *Encyclopædia Britannica,* is nothing short of preposterous.

These editors are first of all scholars, and scholars of the highest rank. To deal with Anglo-Israelism the most outstanding of the theological scholars have been called in and consulted. Naturally, they base their verdict on the Word of God, the Scriptures having been their special study. And yet adherents of British-Israelism have the audacity to ignore their verdict. I insist, my friends, that the statements of the encyclopædias are unanswerable.

British-Israelism Untrue

There are four reasons why I believe British-Israelism to be untrue.

First of all, it is untrue from a *historical* standpoint,

and I quote now from a theologian and Bible teacher of outstanding ability, Rev. Joseph W. Kemp. Let us weigh carefully every word.

"We are asked to believe, forsooth, that nearly three million Israelites poured into Great Britain, and that they dropped their language, physiognomy, customs, records, their names and their memory; and, what is equally astonishing, that for two thousand years nobody seems to have suspected the astounding fact. The thing, of course, never occurred, and I doubt if in the whole world there could be found a historian of any note who would risk his reputation by averring it did. Synagogues and customs (circumcision, for instance) mark today every city to which the Jew has wandered. Further, that an entire race, which once wrote from right to left should, without leaving a single trace of the process behind, revolutionize its penmanship by now writing from left to right, is impossible to conceive."

In the second place, I consider Anglo-Israelism untrue from a *national* standpoint.

"What a travesty of the Kingdom of God British-Israelism presents to the world! British-Israelites claim that Britain is the place of God's appointment, where the ten tribes are to be blessed. If Britain be the place, and the British people Israel, how comes it they shall move no more (2 Sam. 7: 10) when Israel is yet to inhabit the vast territory of Palestine—Mesopotamia? Again, has Britain nothing to fear from the children of wickedness—her enemies? Can anyone possessed of reasoning faculties argue that the promise of David, as quoted, is fulfilled today? For the surrounding nations to be told that the British Empire is the Divine Kingdom on earth, and that the British throne, the Throne of David, to which all nations must ultimately bow, is tragic, and, to the nations concerned, ludicrous and politically dangerous. Is it not clear that a war on Britain by any nation would be war on God?"

In the third place, I consider British-Israelism untrue from an *ecclesiastical* standpoint.

"British-Israel Truth says: 'Israel has been re-coven-anted by being baptized into the one Catholic and Apostolic Church,' and now 'the gospel of salvation must be preached by his constituted agents, the house of Israel'. How can the nation be baptized into the Church and still remain a nation, and simultaneously evangelize all other nations? The Word of God emphatically declares that in the Church 'there is neither Greek nor Jew, circumcision nor uncircumcision, Barbarian, Scythian, bond nor free' (Col. 3: 11). Nationalism within the Church is a complete subversion of Scripture truth regarding the Church. It makes national prosperity and greatness the hall-marks of Divine favour, thus ignoring individual regeneration and sanctity. The inspired division of mankind into 'Jews, Gentiles', and 'the Church of God' (1 Cor. 10: 32) would make Israelites non-existent if they are Jews."

Finally, British-Israelism, I believe to be untrue from a *Biblical* standpoint.

Five Bible Statements

There are five statements in the Word of God that prove conclusively the impossibility of the Anglo-Saxon races being the lost ten tribes.

The first is found in Amos 9: 8-9, where God says: "I will sift the house of Israel among all nations." Therefore no nation on national territory of its own, can be Israel. The Jews have been sifted and scattered among the nations of the world. But British people never have. They are today on their own territory. Hence, Great Britain and the United States cannot be Israel.

From Deuteronomy 28: 62, we understand that the Israelites are to be few in number, and that they are to flee before their enemies (Lev. 26: 17, 36). That has never been true of Great Britain, nor of the United States. The British people are by no means few in number, nor do they flee before their enemies. Hence, they cannot be Israel.

Hosea 3: 4 tells us that they are to remain without a

king, a prince and a sacrifice for many days. That has been true of Israel, for they have had neither king, prince nor sacrifice for nearly two thousand years. But, never has it been true of Great Britain. Hence, Britain is not Israel.

In Numbers 23: 9 we are told that the people of Israel are to dwell alone, and that they are to be unknown among the nations. That prophecy has been fulfilled, so far as the Jews are concerned. For over 2,000 years they were not recognized as a nation. But Great Britain is most certainly reckoned among the nations of the world in a very real sense, and so is the United States.

Last of all, according to Genesis 17: 14, the Israelites were to be barred from blessing unless circumcised. That law has never been changed. All Israelites have to be circumcised. The Anglo-Saxons are not a circumcised people, and, therefore are barred from the blessings promised to Israel.

Why British-Israelism is Untrue

But now to go a little further—just why is it untrue? Well, let me answer by asking five questions, and these five questions are absolutely unanswerable.

1. *To whom were the promises of blessing given?*

According to the Word of God as found in Ezekiel 37: 11, 16, 17–23, they were given to the "whole house of Israel". Not to Judah alone, mark you, but to all twelve tribes. Nowhere does it say that Israel is to enjoy them apart from Judah (Isa. 11: 12, 13; Jer. 3: 18).

2. *In which land were they to be fulfilled?*

In their own land, namely, Palestine. Neither in Britain nor America. There is no promise of blessing for Israel when outside Palestine (Jer. 3: 17–18; Ezek. 36: 28; 37: 22).

3. *When are the promises to be fulfilled?*

Not until the Millennium. There is no prediction that indicates a fulfilment before. Only after Christ has returned and the throne of David set up, will the promises be fulfilled. Not before. (Jer. 23: 5-8; 32: 37-44; Ezek. 37: 24-25).

4. *What is to be Israel's condition until then?*

According to Paul in Romans 11: 5, 7, 11, 25, darkness, blindness and unbelief, except for the election of grace. That prediction is true of the Jews today, but not of either Great Britain or America. Israel is to remain in darkness, blindness and unbelief during the present dispensation.

5. *How long is this to last?*

"Until the fulness of the Gentiles be come in" (Rom. 11: 25). And this one passage from verses 13 to 25, which declares that Israel, and not Judah alone, is to be broken off, and that "blindness in part is happened to Israel, until the fulness of Gentiles be come in", proves conclusively that British-Israelism cannot be true. Israel has been broken off. Israel is blind, and Israel will remain in that condition until the Church has been completed. It does not say Judah, mark you, but Israel.

British-Israelism Dangerous

British-Israelism is dangerous because it places the emphasis on national instead of individual salvation. As Dr. Mountain says "the British people have accepted the Christian faith, and come under the New Covenant".

It is like saying that because a man is a Roman Catholic or a Protestant, a Presbyterian or a Methodist, that therefore he is a Christian. Already there have been suggestions to the effect that if a man is a British-Israelite he is a Christian. And that is exactly the way British-Israelism is heading today. It is national salvation.

Let those who have attended the great soul-winning campaigns and revival services of men like Moody, Chapman, Torrey, Billy Sunday, Gipsy Smith and Billy Graham, go to a meeting of British-Israelites, and note the difference. Is there any invitation? Are sinners urged to leave their seats and come down the aisles to accept Christ as Saviour? Do the British-Israelites have inquiry rooms where their personal workers deal with souls, or is there an altar to which the unsaved are invited? Do they rejoice in the salvation of lost men and women at their meetings?

Or do they simply argue from an intellectual standpoint on behalf of their pet theory, and then sing "God Save the Queen" and disperse? In a word, are they seeking to win Christians to British-Israelism, or sinners to Christ?

Individual Regeneration Necessary

The Apostle Paul knew no such message. He looked upon all men, both Jews and Gentiles, as sinners, and he insisted on individual regeneration. In fact, he turned his back on nationalism, and even spoke of the faith of his forefathers as "the Jews' religion", which he renounced for Christ. There is not a single word that would lead us to believe for a moment that he placed any faith in either Judaism or Israelism.

And, after all, what does it matter? Suppose we are Israelites, we have to be saved just like others. Hence, if men are lost and need a Saviour, why not spend all our time and energy in bringing them to Christ, rather than seeking to persuade them of their Israelitish origin? Our Lord's command was "Go ye into all the world, and preach the gospel to every creature". At no time did He tell us to go into all the world and persuade men of the truth of British-Israelism.

Already there is far too much pride in the heart of man. Men are proud of their ancestry, proud of their nationality, proud of their religion, and it is this pride that has to be rooted out before they can see themselves as common, ordinary sinners, needing a Saviour. To tell them that they are Israelites, entitled to the covenant blessings, is only to add to their pride and to make it much more difficult to persuade them of their need of a Saviour. And it is because British-Israelism does that very thing, that it is so dangerous.

Hence, we would warn the people of God against this, another error, a latter-day heresy, and urge those who are dabbling in it to renounce its absurdities and go on to the deeper things of God.

CHAPTER XVIII

WHO ARE THE SPIRITUALISTS AND WHAT DO THEY TEACH?

SPIRITISM, or Spiritualism, as it is called, originated in the United States through the Fox sisters, in the year 1848. However, it is not new; it is very old, for it has been practised for thousands of years.

Paul definitely predicted it in 1 Timothy 4: 1: "Now the Spirit speaketh expressly, that in the latter times some shall depart from the faith, giving heed to seducing spirits and doctrines of devils."

Most of it is nothing but deception, but some is real, and when it is real, the mediums, or witch doctors, are in contact with, and under control of, demons or evil spirits.

Spiritualist mediums claim that they can communicate with the dead. Let me say that that is absolutely impossible and that no message left by spiritualists has ever reached the living. If the dead can communicate with the living, then why did not the rich man himself communicate with his five brothers? Abraham told him it was impossible (Luke 16: 19–31).

Why it is Wrong

If anyone quotes the incident of the Witch of Endor, just remember that God worked a miracle and brought up Samuel, not the witch, for she was the most surprised of all. And then remember that God destroyed Saul for consulting her, for spiritism was one of the causes of his death. "So Saul died for . . . asking counsel of one that had a familiar spirit, to inquire of it" (1 Chron. 10: 13–14). That shows how dangerous it is.

It was Manasseh's spiritism that provoked God to anger. "He observed times, and used enchantments in the sight of the Lord, to provoke him to anger" (2 Kings 21: 6). That shows how God hates it.

Simon the sorcerer was reproved by Peter for his spiritism. "I perceive that thou art in the gall of bitterness, and in the bond of iniquity" (Acts 8: 23). That shows how sinful it is in the sight of God.

Elymas, the sorcerer who opposed Paul, was struck blind. Here is Paul's denunciation of him: "O full of all subtilty and all mischief, thou child of the devil, thou enemy of all righteousness, wilt thou not cease to pervert the right ways of the Lord?" (Acts 13: 10). That shows how devilish it is.

A damsel who was a spiritualist medium was delivered by God from her spirit control (Acts 16: 16–24). That shows that even a medium can be saved and set free, and that God is opposed to spiritism.

All spiritualists who do not repent are doomed, and doomed forever. "Sorcerers . . . shall have their part in the lake which burneth with fire and brimstone, which is the second death" (Rev. 21: 8). Beware then of spiritism.

Spiritism Condemned

Everywhere in the Word of God spiritism is condemned. How then can Christians have anything to do with it? Let me quote just four passages to prove my assertion:

Deuteronomy 18: 9–14: "There shall not be found among you any that useth divination, or an observer of times, or an enchanter, or a witch, or a charmer, or a consulter with familiar spirits, or a wizard, or a necromancer. For all that do these things are an abomination unto the Lord."

Leviticus 19: 31: "Regard not them that have familiar spirits, neither seek after wizards to be defiled by them."

Leviticus 20: 6: "The soul that turneth after such as have familiar spirits and after wizards, to go a whoring after them, I will even set my face against that soul, and will cut him off from among the people."

Leviticus 20: 27: "A man also or a woman that hath a familiar spirit [a medium], shall surely be put to death:

they shall stone them with stones; their blood shall be upon them." That means that if you are a spiritualist medium, and if you had lived before Christ, you would have been stoned to death.

What fearful denunciations! Yet in spite of what God says there are those who dare to consult spiritualist mediums and to practise the black magic of spiritism.

Spiritism is classed as a false cult because its teachings are utterly unscriptural.

1. *It denies the existence of God*

"There are many Gods. Trees, stars are gods. It is vain to suppose you can serve one God. We abrogate the idea of a personal God."—Wilkins. Does that sound like the Bible? I should say not.

2. *It denies the Fall*

"The Bible account of the fall is a legend and mislead-ing," it says. "Never was there any evidence of a fall."—Conan Doyle. So you see it definitely states that it does not accept the teaching of the Bible regarding the origin of sin. Hence it is unscriptural. How then can a Christian have anything to do with it?

3. *It denies the Virgin Birth*

"The miraculous conception of Christ is merely a fabu-lous tale," it insists. What a contradiction of the Bible record—"conceived of the Holy Ghost" (Matt. 1: 20).

4. *It denies the deity of Christ*

"Jesus Christ was not divine. He was nothing more than a medium in Judea and is now an advanced spirit in the sixth sphere," it states. It does not believe that Christ was the Son of God. "Christ . . . is not the Son of the Creator. Any just and perfect being is Christ," it declares. What paganism. How utterly unscriptural! "Christ was a good man, but He could not have been divine."—Raupert. So man has no Saviour, for Jesus was not divine. Again it is unscriptural, for the Scriptures teach that He was God the Son, as I have stated in my article on Jehovah's Witnesses. That is why a Christian cannot be a spiritualist.

5. *It denies the resurrection*

"Christ arose in spirit. It was the spirit that appeared to the disciples."—Colville. What nonsense! Jesus said "Handle me, and see; for a spirit hath not flesh and bones, as ye see me have" (Luke 24: 39).

6. *It denies the second coming of Christ*

"There will be no such personal return as theologians have taught."—Colville. "The coming of Christ commenced about 1847—a coming of ministering angels and spirits."—What rubbish! What a travesty on the plain scriptural teaching concerning the return of Christ. "This same Jesus which is taken up from you into heaven, shall so come in like manner as ye have seen him go into heaven" (Acts 1: 11).

7. *It denies salvation by the atoning blood of Christ*

That is the most damning denial of all, for the Bible proclaims salvation by blood from Genesis to Revelation, and in no other way. But this is what spiritism says about it:

"Future bliss is not by faith in notions of atonement and vicarious sacrifice, but by merit that man lays up for himself by slow and laborious process."

"Man is his own priest and saviour."

"The whole doctrine of original sin, the fall, the vicarious atonement, the placation of the Almighty by blood—all this is abhorrent."

"There is no atoning value in the death of Christ."

What blasphemy! But no wonder they hate the blood, for they are unsaved, unregenerated, lost and hopeless. They deal in demonism and they have no light. Not one verse of Scripture can they produce for their bloodless teachings. They are only their own Christ-rejecting opinions. Theirs is the heresy of Cain. No wonder they are doomed. God help the Christian who seeks their help.

8. *It denies the personality of the Holy Spirit*

"There is no such thing as a personal Holy Spirit," it declares. But the Bible says there is, so again it is unscriptural.

9. *Finally, it denies the resurrection of the dead, future judgment, the devil and hell*

"There is no resurrection and no judgment," it states. "There is no hell and no devil. Hell does not exist and never will."—Conan Doyle.

Well, that is clear enough. Words could not be plainer. Yet these are the truths that are set forth in the Bible in no uncertain way. The Bible says there is to be a resurrection and also a judgment. That the devil and hell are real. But they do not believe the Bible, even though it says, "After death the judgment" (Heb. 9: 27).

An Infernal Demon

Read these words from Dr. B. P. Randolph, who for a brief time forsook Spiritualism and made these statements in a lecture in New York City—"For seven years I held daily intercourse with what was purported to be my mother's spirit, an infernal demon, who in that guise gained my soul's confidence and led me to the brink of ruin. Five of my friends destroyed themselves and I attempted it, by direct spiritual influences. Every crime in the calendar has been committed by mortals moved by viewless beings. I have a volume of sixty closely-written pages of names of those who have been drawn from respectability, morality, wealth and intelligence, to the filth of free love, poverty and insanity itself . . . It changes man's worship of God to a worship of ghosts."

My friends, I have not taken time to quote Scripture to answer them, since everything they teach is utterly contrary to the Word. And everything they deny is taught in the Bible. But even if I did, they would not accept it, for they do not believe the Bible to be the authoritative, infallible Word of God. "There is much in the Bible," they say, "which does not amalgamate with our teaching." No wonder they hate it.

"The world is full of false prophets. You can test them in this simple way: every spirit that acknowledges the fact that Jesus, God's Christ, actually became Man, comes from God, but the spirit which denies this fact does not come from God" (1 John 4: 1–3—Phillips).

May the Holy Spirit open their blind eyes before it is forever too late, and save them lest they perish. I would point them to Isaiah 53: 6, Hebrews 9: 22, Leviticus 17: 11, 1 Peter 1: 19, Romans 6: 23, John 1: 12; 3: 14–18, 36; 5: 24. Their only hope of salvation is in the vicarious atoning death of Jesus Christ on Calvary's cross.